Analysis & Study Guide: Songs of Innocence and Experience

Francis Gilbert

Francis Gilbert

Copyright © 2020 Francis Gilbert
This edition first published in 2020 by FGI publishing, London
www.francisgilbert.co.uk

All rights reserved.
ISBN 9781913694005

Songs of Innocence and Experience: A Study Guide

Contents

Dedication 6

Acknowledgements 6

Also by Francis Gilbert 6

Introduction 7

Biography: Blake's life 8

Biography in brief 12

Questions to ask if you want to develop a personal response 15

Developing an academic response 20

Analysing Language 22

Key concepts 30

Blake on the internet 32

The Bible 34

Title pages 45

Introduction (Innocence) 46

The Shepherd 51

The Ecchoing Green 54

The Lamb 57

The Little Black Boy 60

The Blossom 63

The Chimney Sweeper 65

The Little Boy Lost (Innocence) 69

The Little Boy Found (Innocence) 70

The Laughing Song 72

A Cradle Song 74

The Divine Image (Innocence) 78

Holy Thursday (Innocence) 81
Night 84
Spring 88
Nurse's Song (Innocence) 90
Infant Joy 92
A Dream 94
On Another's Sorrow 97
Songs of Experience – Title page 102
Introduction to Experience 102
Earth's Answer 103
The Clod & the Pebble 108
Holy Thursday (Experience) 110
The Little Girl Lost and Found (Experience) 113
The Little Girl Found 115
The Chimney Sweeper (Experience) 119
Nurse's Song (Experience) 122
The Sick Rose 124
The Fly 126
The Angel 128
The Tyger 130
My Pretty Rose Tree, Ah! Sun-Flower, The Lilly 135
My Pretty Rose Tree 136
Ah! Sun-flower 136
The Lilly 136
The Garden of Love 139
The Little Vagabond 142
London 145

The Human Abstract 150

Infant Sorrow 154

A Poison Tree 156

A Little Boy Lost (Experience) 158

A Little Girl Lost (Second poem in Experience) 161

To Tirzah 163

The School Boy 166

The Voice of the Ancient Bard 169

A Divine Image (Experience) 170

How to do well when writing about Blake's poetry 172

Find the poem which goes with the "contextual" quote or comment. 172

Common themes in Blake's poetry 175

Comparing Blake with other texts 176

Questions to help you compare the poems 177

How to write a good essay on Blake 179

Bibliography 186

About the author 187

Dedication

To my inspiring Year 13 classes who worked valiantly to understand the complexities of this great visionary writer.

Acknowledgements

First, huge thanks must go to my wife, Erica Wagner, for always supporting me with my writing and teaching. Second, I'm very grateful to all the students and teachers who have helped me write this book. Any mistakes in the book are entirely mine and they have no responsibility for them whatsoever!

Also by Francis Gilbert

I'm A Teacher, Get Me Out Of Here (2004)
Teacher On The Run (2005)
Yob Nation (2006)
Parent Power (2007)
Working The System: How To Get The Very State Education For Your Child (2011)
The Last Day Of Term (2012)
Gilbert's Study Guides on: *Frankenstein, Far From The Madding Crowd, The Hound of the Baskervilles , Pride and Prejudice, The Strange Case of Dr Jekyll and Mr Hyde, The Turn of the Screw, Wuthering Heights & How to Get a Great English Degree* (2013)

Songs of Innocence and Experience: A Study Guide

Introduction

Why did I write this guide?
First, it's for my own benefit; I find writing about subjects I love (and have to teach) helps me understand them better.

Second, I believe the guide could really help both students and teachers. Having scanned for materials on Blake on the internet, I can see that there's an awful lot of stuff which is, quite frankly, "anti-Blakean". William Blake believed in the power of the human imagination; he hated systems which "prescribed" ways of doing things. He hated unfair laws and codes. Much of what I read on the internet seems to be saying "you must interpret Blake in this way otherwise you'll fail your exam!". Blake hated the idea of school exams – he writes powerfully about the horrors of school in *The School Boy* – and would have really hated the idea that his poems had to be interpreted in ONE particular way; indeed, I've included links in this guide to the multiple illustrated versions he did of the poems – he coloured them quite differently from version to version, and sometimes changed words.

What I wanted to do with this guide was devise one which is "Blakean" in spirit, a guide which gave the reader enough information and confidence to interpret the poems for him or herself: this is why I have included both "pre-reading" questions, which will get students thinking about key themes in the poems, and "creative response questions", which aim to get students responding in an imaginative fashion to the verse.
Francis Gilbert, November 2013, sir@francisgilbert.co.uk

Biography: Blake's life

William Blake was born in 1757 in Soho, London. He was the son of a "hosier" -- a merchant who sold stockings and other garments. His family was part of an emerging "artisan" class in London; this is a group of people who were making their living by selling products they made, but also had views on things which were often at odds with the ruling classes, the monarchy and aristocracy. Blake's family, like Blake himself, were "non-conformists", that is, they called themselves Christians but did not accept the established church as interpreting Christ's teachings correctly. This was a big deal at the time because everyone was religious and most people attended traditional church services, going to established churches to pray, to get married, to get their children baptized. Non-conformists rejected many of the views of the established church and interpreted the Bible in their own way, often holding their services in places like ale-houses – something Blake refers to in the *The Little Vagabond*. Some non-conformist believed that the church was actually the "devil" or the "beast" – referred to in *Revelations* in the Bible – and saw many of its beliefs as evil. It's not difficult to see how Blake was "non-conformist" in much of his poetry: in the *Songs of Experience*, you'll see again and again how he attacks the church for setting rules which destroy the natural joys of childhood (see *The Garden of Love*) and for doing things like employing slave labour (see *London*).

Blake's family were then religious in a different way to many people. They questioned, like many artisans who lived in the area, the values, the views and the policies of the ruling classes. The young William was a gifted and exceptional child. He had a vision of God at the age of four, and later on he saw a tree full of angels in a field at Peckham Rye. When he told his mother about this, she thought he was lying and beat him. However, the visions continued for the rest of his life; some people like the biographer Peter Ackroyd have speculated that he had an "eidetic imagination". In other words, he had the ability to see things at will, even if they weren't there. After being taught to read on his mother's knee, his father perceived his son's artistic talents and paid for him to attend Henry Parr's drawing school for three years. After this, Blake became an apprentice to the engraver, James Basire, who was the engraver to the London Society of Antiquaries. At this time, Blake was also writing poetry as well as learning to be an artist and engraver. As part of his training, he was allowed into Westminster Abbey and carried out drawings of the effigies in the Abbey on behalf of Basire. The architecture and art in the Abbey had a profound effect upon Blake; you can see many of its influences in his pictures. You have to understand that Blake lived in a time when there were virtually no free galleries for ordinary people to view art; it was only the very rich who got to see collections of art. Other people's only chance to look at art was usually in church.

Having established himself as a very talented engraver with Basire, Blake began to study at the top artistic institution, the Royal Academy. He also began to do engravings for the radical publisher Joseph Johnson, who published the writings of revolutionary figures like Thomas Paine, who wrote a book called *The Rights of Man* which argued that all men were equal and were entitled to equal rights. This was a dangerous idea at the time because most people accepted that the monarchy and the ruling class were just naturally better than them. In 1780, Blake witnessed a huge riot which saw the hated Newgate Prison – now the Old Bailey – burned down. Some biographers argue that Blake joined in with the rioting, but others think he hung back, watching the buildings burn. The riots lasted six days. A little later, Blake and some friends were arrested on the river Medway after sketching what turned out to be a military installation. They were freed when it was clear that they weren't French spies. What we realize from both these incidents is that the authorities in England were very nervous; the ruling classes were very worried that they would be overthrown by the people, who were, in the main, very poor and desperate.

In 1782, Blake fell in love with a girl who rejected him but he found comfort in the arms of another girl, Catherine Boucher, the daughter of a Battersea market-gardener. She took pity on him and he fell in love with her. He married her even though it wasn't an "advantageous" marriage in that she was very poor and brought no "dowry" with her. But the union was a great success: Blake moulded Catherine in his own image, teaching her how to read, write and to print. They had no children, but the marriage seems to have been a happy one, although some biographers believe that Blake's views on free love angered his wife, and have interpreted some of the explorations of sexuality in his writing as frustration at his marital situation.

Blake began to write the first poems which were to form the *Songs of Innocence* a couple of years after getting married. This was at a time when he had great hopes for his future; he was getting quite a bit of work as an engraver. This largely meant that he copied other people's paintings onto metal plates that were then printed in magazines and books; sometimes he would draw an original picture. During the 1780-90s, he believed he could make his name as a poet and artist in his own right. He published his *Poetical Sketches* in 1783, and even though he didn't sell any copies, he began work on the *Songs of Innocence* in 1784. Although he never was commercially successful with his poetry, he often had a group of friends and acquaintances who appreciated his work; he would sing his poems at various gatherings.

In 1787, the most devastating event of his life occurred when his beloved brother Robert died. Blake nursed his brother, who had tuberculosis, for two weeks without sleep before he died. At the moment of his death, Blake saw Robert's spirit rising through the ceiling, clapping his hands for joy. From then on, he used Robert's sketch-book to make notes and draft poems. He wrote later on that the spirit of his brother was with him every minute of the day. A while later, he had a dream about Robert, who told him how to print his *Songs of Innocence*; showing him in the dream an innovative method of etching called "relief etching". This was the idea that you wrote on a metal plate with a sort of glue or varnish and then bathed the metal plate in acid, which would eat away at everything that was not varnished, thus leaving the words and picture sticking out in relief. This was the reverse of the normal method of etching because usually what the artist painted was the bit that was eaten away by the acid so that the picture was dug out of the plate. At about this time, Blake became very interested in the ideas of Swedenborg who was a spiritual Christian who believed in the existence of spirits on earth, claiming that the dead walked among us. Later Blake would reject many of Swedenborg's ideas but the belief in spirits remained because it tied in with his own visions and experiences.

In 1790, he moved to Lambeth, across the river from Soho, away from the noisy city and loved living in a house with a garden, where he used to walk naked. Blake was a nudist, believing that everyone had the right to walk around as they were created, naked. This was an enormously productive period for him, he wrote many poems, long and short ones, and he worked furiously on many commissions. He believed that he could be a successful artist. He published his *Songs of Innocence and Experience* in 1794 and hoped to sell a number of copies, but very few were bought. A year later, he was attacked and robbed in the street; work began to be very hard to come by and he would have struggled to stay alive if it hadn't been for a wealthy patron, Thomas Butts, who asked Blake to engrave a number of pictures based on Blake's favourite Biblical and literary subjects. In 1800, he moved to Sussex to work for the poet William Hayley; he had hoped that the move would enable him to write more poetry and become more successful as an artist. Unfortunately, the whole venture turned into a disaster because he found Hayley very patronizing and the cottage where he lived in Felpham was very damp and gave Catherine a bad cough. In 1803, he kicked out a drunken soldier, Schofield, from his garden who then accused Blake of saying terrible things about the king, a crime which was called sedition and which carried a very heavy prison sentence or possibly meant the death penalty. With no money and with the threat of the trial hanging over his head, Blake returned to London in dire poverty, all his dreams of a better life shattered. In 1804, he returned to Sussex for his trial at Chichester

Quarter Sessions; mercifully he was acquitted to the cheers of the gallery who realized the injustice of the charge.

From this time onwards, Blake really struggled to make his living as an engraver, surviving on very little work near where he grew up in London. However, in 1824 when Blake was getting old, a young group of artists called the Ancients befriended him and modeled much of their art on his, particularly his work depicting rural scenes, which you can see some of at the beginning of the *Songs of Innocence* in the illustrations to the *Introduction* to the *Songs of Innocence*, *The Shepherd*, *The Ecchoing Green* and *The Lamb*. Blake became much calmer and less bitter about his treatment in his later years, and died in 1827 singing about his visions of heaven.

Biography in brief

1757 William, the second of four children, is born at 28 Broad Street, Soho.

1761 At age four, Blake had a vision of God; later he saw a tree full of angels in a field at Peckham Rye.

1767 Robert Blake, his favourite brother is born.

1768 After being taught at home, Blake attends Henry Pars's Drawing school for three years.

1769 He writes his *Poetical Sketches*, a brilliant collection of poems still anthologized today.

1772 He becomes an apprentice to James Basire, engraver to London Society of Antiquaries.

1773 He engraves his first picture *Joseph of Arimathea* after a figure in Michelangelo's *The Crucifixion of St. Peter*.

1774 He makes drawings for Basire in Westminster Abbey and sees the disinterment of Edward 1.

1779 Begins study at the Royal Academy under G. M. Moser, does engravings for the radical publisher Joseph Johnson, who publishes the work of many radical thinkers like Paine and Wollstonecraft.

1780 First exhibit at the Royal Academy. Witnesses the Gordon

Riots of June 2-8 and sees the burning of Newgate Prison. Taken prisoner with other artists after being mistaken for a French spy while sketching on the Medway river.

1782 Marries Catherine Boucher, the daughter of a Battersea market-gardener. He teaches Catherine to read, write and make prints; they have no children throughout their long marriage.

1783 Publishes his *Poetical Sketches*, but no copies sold. He sings his poems to his friends and colleagues, which he continued to do throughout his life.

1784 The first of the *Songs of Innocence* is written.

1785 A print shop set up with a colleague fails, then Blake moves to Poland Street. He exhibits at the Royal Academy.

1787 After looking after his brother for two weeks without sleep, Robert Blake dies of tuberculosis. At the moment of his death, Blake saw Robert's spirit rising through the ceiling, clapping his hands for joy. He begins using Robert's sketch-book to make notes/draft poems.

1788 Becomes interested in the spiritual Christianity of Swedenborg, who believed in the existence of spirits which are part of everyone.

1789 Writes and illustrates the *Songs of Innocence* after Robert visits him in a dream and shows him how to print the poems himself using the innovative "relief" printing method. Begins to work on other illuminated books which explore political, religious and spiritual themes.

1790 Moves to Lambeth, away from the congested city and enjoys living in a house with garden. Enjoys walking around naked; he believes every person has the right to walk around naked.

1794 Publishes *Songs of Innocence and Experience*.

1795 He is "mobbed and robbed".

1799 Work is very hard to come by. He is rescued by Thomas Butts who commissions a number of engravings on Biblical and literary subjects.

1800-3 He moves to Sussex to work for William Hayley, drawing *the Heads of Poets*.

1803 He evicts a drunk soldier, Scofield, from his garden and is accused by Scofield of uttering seditious threats against the King. Returns to London in dire poverty.

1804 Put on trial for sedition but is acquitted at Chichester Quarter Sessions to the cheers of spectators.

1805-8 Struggles as an engraver. His ideas are possibly plagiarized by other artists. Becomes very angry and bitter at his treatment.

1824 As an old man, he befriends some much younger artists who marvel at his art. Enters a new phase of calm.

1827 Dies aged 69 at 6pm August 12, singing about what he saw in heaven.

Further reading

Ackroyd, P. *Blake* (1999) Vintage, London.

This is, without doubt, the most compelling biography of Blake. It is written like a historical novel; it is full of colour about Blake's life and times. You can smell the streets, you can taste the food, you can see Blake's visions. This is Ackroyd's masterpiece and a brilliant piece of work.

Bedard, M. *William Blake: The Gates of Paradise* (2006) Tundra Books, New York.

Bedard's short biography is handsomely produced and is very readable. For me, it is the best short life of Blake because it draws on recent research into Blake's life.

Gilchrist, A & Holmes, R. *Gilchrist on Blake – Classic Biographies edited by Richard Holmes.* (1863/2005) Harper Perennial, London.

This is the first biography of Blake published in 1863. The well-known biographer Richard Holmes provides a fascinating introduction to this edition in which he shows how Gilchrist's biography managed to bring Blake's work to the attention of the public. The story of its writing was an exciting and sad one: Gilchrist was a young man who was passionate about Blake's work and tracked down people who remembered Blake, interviewing them at length, but died before he could complete his biography.

Fortunately, his wife finished it for him, finding invaluable extra material as she did so.

For a good time line of his life, log onto: http://www.crossref-it.info/textguide/Songs-of-Innocence-and-Experience/13/Timeline or watch: https://www.youtube.com/watch?v=v3hQXQ5_zCM

Questions to ask if you want to develop a personal response

Above all, you need to develop a personal response to Blake's poems. To do this, you need to ask the right sort of questions of Blake's work and answer them for yourself. This study guide can only point you in the right direction, it cannot and should not give you all the answers.

The first question you could ask is:

What effects are created when the poem is read aloud or sung?

For me, this is THE most important question. William Blake calls his poems "songs"; he clearly intended them to be sung – or thought of as being sung, even when read silently. There is some evidence that he himself sung the songs. You might not want to sing the songs, but you should at least have a go at saying them out aloud with expression. You may be surprised at what you hear: hopefully, you'll hear the music of the poems. In my study guide, I've included internet links to readings and sung versions of the poems where possible. I myself have had a go at setting the poems to music and singing them, though I must stress that I am by no means a professional musician or singer -- I'm actually not very good! But I've put them on the internet in a "Blakean" spirit; the spirit of experimentation and provocation. If you don't like what I've done, do better yourself – I'm sure you can! Read the poems out aloud with real feeling! Get drumming! Get singing! The poems are NOT there to be analysed to death, they are there to be SUNG! Don't worry too much about understanding every word. This isn't how poetry works. Poetry works when it creates mystery and atmosphere, when it provokes thoughts and feelings. Poetry dies when it is "over-analysed" – as Wordsworth said, "We murder to dissect". It is supposed to be enjoyed.

The second question you could ask is:

What questions do you have about the poem?

This seems crucial too. These poems raise more questions than answers. There is so much in them that is mysterious. Rather than seeking answers, we need to ask questions. And this I feel is exactly what Blake would have wanted. It is, actually, what most teachers and examiners want too. Essays which are full of certainty about Blake's poetry are MISSING THE POINT!!

The third question you could ask is:

What interests you most about the poem? Why?

Again, a vital question if you're going to develop a personal response to the poem – which any good discussion will do. Don't be suckered in by the study guides that pretend to offer the definitive interpretation of the poem; there's a lot of criticism of William Blake that needs to be taken with a big pinch of salt. There's a great deal that we DON'T KNOW about what he meant when he wrote the poems; some critics have seen him as a mystic who coded secret messages into his poems, while others have viewed him as writing like a Romantic poet, rather like William Wordsworth. While these interpretations are interesting to read, they're not necessarily THE way to view Blake. It's far better to look at the lines that interest you and discuss them with people in your class, and work out in detail WHY the lines interest you. You might use the 5Ws to help you with this:

WHAT language is interesting?

WHO is speaking at this point in the poem?

WHEN does the language change in tone and atmosphere?

WHERE is the poem set?

WHY is the language interesting?

I discuss Blake's poem, 'The Sick Rose' on YouTube and explore how you might use the 5Ws to discuss a poem here:
http://www.youtube.com/watch?v=p7vqS58arHU

The fourth question I ask is:

Songs of Innocence and Experience: A Study Guide

What is the poem about?

Any good answer will include a decent explanation of what the reader imagines is going on in the poem, backed up by textual evidence to justify his/her claims. As a teacher, I read too many critiques of poems which don't contain this; many students wade straight into analyzing the literary techniques of a poem, without considering what is actually going on in it.

The fifth question I ask is:

What effects does the language create?

Any good literary analysis of poetry explores the EFFECTS of the language of a poem; that is what the language makes you THINK, what it makes you FEEL, what it makes you IMAGINE. All language has an EFFECT upon a reader, it provokes thought, feelings and imaginings. It's very useful to consider the CONNOTATIONS of the language; the THOUGHTS, the FEELINGS, the IMAGININGS it provokes in your mind. When you explore the CONNOTATIONS of a poem, you're beginning to explore the poem's literary techniques because you're thinking about the sorts of FEELINGS, THOUGHTS and IMAGININGS that the writer may be trying to provoke in a reader's mind.

A key point is to find THE ORIGINAL transcript of the poem. So many versions of Blake's poems on the web TIDY UP the spellings, and add in extra punctuation. I think it's very important to look at them in the original because this is how Blake intended them to be read. He lived in a time when "standardization" of spelling and punctuation wasn't really in existence; people could spell and punctuate pretty much as they wanted. He was actually very much against standardization. You can find the originals of the poems here:

http://www.concordancesoftware.co.uk/webconcordances/blake/framconc.htm

The sixth question I ask is:

What is the effect of the poem's structure and form?

This is a question that is particularly important about poetry because the form of poetry is all about STRUCTURE. Blake, and many other poets, STRUCTURES his poems so that they use

RHYTHM and RHYME to create certain EFFECTS. The RHYTHM of a poem can only be understood by reading it aloud and drumming out a beat to it; you need to think carefully about the EFFECT the rhythm creates; it's useless saying that a poem has an "iambic" or "trochaic" rhythm if you don't explain the EFFECT the rhythm has. Likewise, pointing out the rhyme scheme of a poem is pointless unless you're beginning to think about WHY certain words rhyme. Most rhythm and rhyme is there to EMPHASIZE certain ideas, moods, feelings, images and meanings. It's all about EMPHASIS.

The seventh question I ask is:

What are the similarities and differences between other texts?

This is very relevant to the *Songs of Innocence and Experience* because Blake is clearly inviting the reader to make direct comparisons between poems, and to make links between the illustrations and his poems. If you're studying these poems for coursework, you may be asked to make comparisons between other texts as well.

The eighth question I ask is:

How do other people interpret this poem? Find sources/links...

Do some research but look carefully at your sources! Remember Wikipedia entries can be unreliable, check out their links. It's far better to look at reputable sources such the books suggested in the Bibliography at the end of the study guide.

The ninth question I ask is:

What might make a good creative response to the poem?

Blake probably would have hated the idea of a study guide for his poetry; he was a non-conformist who believed that most voices of authority were suspect. But he would have approved of people responding to his poems with poems, stories, paintings, music and film. If you feel so inspired, draw a picture in response to a poem, write a piece of music, or another poem...

My tenth question is:

How might you teach this poem?

For me, this is relevant to both teachers and students. You learn best when you teach a topic to another person. So think about how you might teach a particular poem to someone else.

I have had a go at answering these questions for the first poem in the collection, the *Introduction to Innocence*, to give you an idea about how they might be answered, but for the rest of the poems I've shortened the list of questions because these questions are really for you, the reader, to answer, not me. For the purposes of the study guide, I've tried to answer more academic questions:

MEANING: What is the poem about? This is obviously vital, if you don't know what the possible meanings of the poem are, then you're going to be stuck.

CONTEXTS: What possibly influenced the writing of the poem? How we might read the poem now? The whole question of the "contexts" of a poem is a tricky one, but vital. There are two major types of context: contexts of writing and contexts of reading. The contexts of writing are circumstances and situations in which a poem was written in; this often can really help you understand and appreciate a text in a much more rewarding fashion. This is particularly true of Blake; when you know a little bit about his life and the times he lived in, you really see how revolutionary he was. Contexts of reading is how we read a text now; this is crucial too and in a sense the ONLY way in which you read a poem. You bring your own unique context to the reading of a text: your age, your gender, your ethnicity, your beliefs, your social class, your education, your geographical location all will affect profoundly how you read a poem. Equally, it's interesting to see how other readers have read Blake's poems.

TECNIQUES and EFFECTS: What linguistic and poetic devices does the poem use and what are their effects? Blake was a master craftsman; he shaped and honed his poetry to create certain effects; he wanted his poetry to provoke feelings, thoughts and images. You will need to look carefully at his poetic techniques and their effects to fully appreciate his poetry.

I have answered these questions for *The Shepherd*, but thereafter I have "integrated" my points about all of these issues into a more sustained piece of writing because ultimately that's what you should be aiming for; an integrated piece of writing which explores the relevant ideas you want to discuss in a fluent, clear and readable fashion. "Check-listing" points can make your writing sound very robotic and functional and certainly would have been something that Blake would have hated.

Developing an academic response

Some of my students who have read a first draft of my study guide have found my language quite academic; that is, the guide, at times, uses sophisticated language and terminology to analyse Blake's poetry. I have thought about simplifying this language, but have decided against this for the reason that I believe it is important to model what an academic response might look like. The trouble is that when you simplify the language, you can dilute your analysis and not convey the complexity of a point. If you are finding the guide difficult to understand at times, can you please get a dictionary and look up the difficult words, and learn what they mean. This will significantly improve your chances of getting a good grade. If we look at what the exam board OCR consider to be the criteria for getting a top grade in a piece of coursework on Blake, we can see that using academic language is a big part of it:

Upper Band 4 (26–30)
- use of framework(s) illuminates textual interpretation
- shows an overview of the text
- engages closely with the meaning of the texts and analyses patterns
- conceptualised and often sophisticated analysis
- fluent, cohesive writing

Upper band 4 (26–30)
- assimilates and contextualises references with originality
- overview that offers observations on wider contexts
- significant similarities and differences are analysed and in an

original, personal, or conceptual manner
- texts effortlessly integrated
- consistent and flexible focus on texts and theme

OCR talk about using a "framework" to illuminate textual interpretation: this essentially means using academic terminology. They also require "sophisticated analysis" which has an "overview" of a text. I read too many answers that plunge into the "micro-analysis" of a poem without doing this; you need to show that you understand the poem overall, by explaining in your own words what you think it is about. You will need to integrate quotation into the main body of your essay, explaining what the surrounding words mean; this is called "contextualising references". You will show also that you can compare the similarities and differences of a text in an "original, personal or conceptual" manner; in other words, you will be arriving at your own responses which fully justified and explained.

Really good answers on Blake will tackle the ways in which he uses poetic techniques. This means getting to grips with the ways in which uses poetic form and things like metaphor, metonymy, and rhythm and rhyme: I have covered these topics below.

Francis Gilbert

Analysing Language

The following exercises are devised by me to help you improve your analysis of language but based on my reading of an extremely useful book: *Reading poetry: an introduction* by Furniss and Bath.

Figurative Language – The Acid Test

"Figurative Language" is a general term for a group of linguistic devices called "figures of speech" (p. 146, Furniss).

A word, phrase or statement is figurative when it cannot be taken literally in the context in which it is being used, for example: "love is blind", or "look before you leap" = could be literal and figurative.

Figurative or not?

"The light at the end of the tunnel"

"The glass half full"

Well, it all depends upon the context. If you are really in a tunnel and you can see a light in front of you, then it's not figurative at all but literal, but if you are struggling with a problem and you begin to see how to solve it, you may say a phrase like there's light at the end of the tunnel, making your language figurative. The same applies with "the glass half full"; you could literally be looking at a glass half full of water, or talking about your situation in life and figuratively describing it that way.

Metonymy and Synecdoche

Metonymy means "change of name"; it is a figure of speech in which the name of one thing is used to name something which is associated with it – as in "the pen is mightier than the sword". This is not literally true. "Pen" means "writing or writers".

E.g. "The White House denied rumours" = the White House represents the government

A figure which is related to metonymy is "synecdoche". Synecdoche works mainly through two associative principles: 'part of the whole' and 'container for contained'. E.g. 'All hands on decks' does not literally mean chopped off hands to be on deck, it means the sailors etc...

"Metaphor *creates* the relation between its objects, while **metonymy** *presupposes* that relation." (Hugh Bredin, "Metonymy." *Poetics Today*, 1984)

Examples

"The suits on Wall Street walked off with most of our savings."

Wall Street = metonymy because it stands in for stockbrokers and bankers

"Lend me your ears..."

Ears = synecdoche because one small object (ears) stands in for a bigger whole (your body)

"He loves the bottle"

Bottle = metonymy because the bottle represents alcohol.

"He is loyal to the crown"

Crown = synecdoche because one small object represents the whole of the monarchy.

Blake uses metonymy and synecdoche quite a bit, and often to great effect. If you look at a poem like *London*, you can see that he employs metonymy when he talks about the blood of the hapless soldier running down the "Palace walls". The "Palace walls" is metonymic because it represents the monarchy and oligarchic government which was sending thousands of soldiers to their deaths by ordering them to fight in various wars.

Metaphor

Metaphor is quite simply when one thing is compared to another without any "like" or "as" in between: "the sun has got his hat on"; "the boxer was a bear"; "his anger was volcanic". It works on the assumption that there are similarities between things. Used in all kinds of language.

All discourses have their own characteristic metaphors.

Analysis of metaphor

Tenor = what is being talked about
Vehicle = the metaphorical way it's being talked about

Ground = the similarities between tenor and vehicle/connotations of the metaphor

E.g. An Englishman's home is his castle

Tenor (what is being talked about) = "an Englishman's home"

Vehicle (metaphorical term) = "his castle"

Ground = the similarities between the tenor and vehicle (e.g. Englishman is lord and master, safe in his home)

Work out these ones

The classroom was a bear-pit

The cesspit of humanity

Answers

The classroom was a bear pit

Tenor = classroom

Vehicle = bear pit

Ground = the classroom is being personified as a wild animal, connoting ill-discipline, poor behavior etc.

The cesspit of humanity

Tenor = humanity

Vehicle = cesspit

Ground = suggesting that people, humans, are like a sewer, dirty, corrupt etc.

Dead Metaphor and Poetic Metaphor

Shelley in *A Defence of Poetry* (1821): "Poetry lifts the veil from the hidden beauty of the world, makes familiar objects be as if they were not familiar". This is very similar to the Russian Formalists' concept of "defamiliarisation".

Defamiliarization is an artistic technique, used in poetry and novels, to force the reader to see an ordinary situation in an entirely different way. For example, Kafka "defamiliarized" the way we see officials and bureaucracy in novels like *The Trial* by telling the story of a man, K, who is arrested but never told why he is arrested, and instead spends most of his time being passed from one official to another. Science fiction often defamiliarises ordinary situations by setting them in a different context. Some critics have argued that Orwell's *1984* is really about the privations of post-war Europe rather being the science fiction novel it purports to be.

Look at these lines and say whether you can work out:
The tenor
The vehicle
The ground
Whether the image is "dead" or "poetic":
> "Shall I compare thee to a summer's day?"
> "You are the light in my life!"

Answers

You could argue that both images are "dead" because although Shakespeare's famous opening line to his sonnet "Shall I compare thee to a summer's day" was once original, it is now so commonly said that it has lost its power. It once was "poetic" but is no longer. The other phrase, "You are the light of my life!" is a cliché and too familiar to be treated as "poetic".

Blake is constantly "defamiliarizing" familiar situations in his poems. For example, he often invests ordinary objects and animals with special meanings and significance; a village green becomes the "ecchoing green", a lamb become a symbol for innocence and joy, trees signify mystery and secrecy, London's streets are invested with terror and misery and so on.

Poetic symbol

The New Princeton Encyclopedia of Poetry and Poetics (1993) says that poetic symbol is "a kind of figurative language in which what is shown (normally referring to something material) means, by virtue of some sort of resemblance, suggestion or association, something more or something else (normally immaterial)". There is a specific "tenor" but it is not certain what the 'vehicle' is, there is no specific reference.

The Symbolist movement focused upon the suggestive power of Symbols.

Look at this poem by William Blake and think about how and why it is a symbolic poem:

Francis Gilbert

> O Rose thou art sick.
> The invisible worm,
> That flies in the night
> In the howling storm:
>
> Has found out thy bed
> Of crimson joy:
> And his dark secret love
> Does thy life destroy.

This poem has been much written about because ultimately we don't know what the "tenor" – what is being talked about – actually is. Clearly, the "Rose" is not a real rose, it is a "vehicle" of some sort but the tenor is never fully explained. As a result, we can only speculate about possible "tenors" and this can lead to some rich, complex and speculative criticism. The specific "tenor" is missing and consequently makes the poem symbolic.

Rhythm

Definitions: prosody = the study of rhythm in poetry, sometimes called metrical analysis.

Rhythm is the BEAT of language: it is the most important element of language when combined with meaning. You could say that rhythm is the heart-beat of language.

In order to "get" the rhythm of a poem you should:

Read the poem out aloud.

Then clap out the rhythm.

Then think about the effects of the rhythm: what does it make you think, feel and see? What is the difference between rhythm and rhyme?

Rhythm = the beat of the poem, where the hard and soft stresses go.

Rhyme = is where there are similar sounds, usually vowel sounds, that chime together, e.g. blue shoe poo you.

The most important thing with rhythm and rhyme is to discuss the **effects** they create: what mood does the rhythm create? What ideas/themes/images/emotions does it emphasize or highlight?

There are two major types of rhythm: rising rhythm and falling rhythm.

Rising rhythm is created by two major types of "stress patterns" or metrical feet: iambs and anapaests. An iamb is a metrical feet which consists of a soft beat followed by a hard one: di-DUM. It is the most common kind of rhythm found in poetry and speech. If we go back to the opening line of Shakespeare's famous sonnet we can see how the line is iambic, when read aloud you can hear how the stresses fall where I have marked the syllables in bold:

> Shall **I** com**pare** thee **to** a **sum**mer's **day**?

The other type of rising rhythm is the anapaest which consists of two soft stresses followed by a hard stress: di-di-DUM. One of William Blake's most rhythmically joyous poems is called *Laughing Song* from the *Songs of Innocence*. This poem really works when you read it aloud and clap the rhythm: it is genuinely like a song; you can just imagine a drum beat making the poem come alive. The poem is largely "anapaestic"; that is, it is full of fast-paced metrical feet called anapaests which create a fantastically energetic tone; the rhythm is always "rising". Let's look at the first verse, the heavy beats are in bold:

> When the **green** woods **laugh** with the **voice** of **joy** (anapest, iamb, anapest, iamb)
> And the **dimpling stream** runs **laugh**ing **by**, (anapest, iamb, iamb, iamb)
> When the **air** does **laugh** with our **mer**ry **wit**, (anapest, iamb, anapest, iamb)
> And the **green** hill **laughs** with the **noise** of **it**. (anapest, iamb, anapest, iamb)

Falling rhythm. The other type of rhythm is the falling rhythm which creates often the sensation of "falling" because the hard stress comes first and is followed by a soft stress. A trochee consists of a hard beat followed by a soft one: DUM-di. William Blake's *The Lamb* is a classic example of this:

> **Lit**tle **Lamb** who **made** thee
> **Dost** thou **know** who **made** thee
> **Gave** thee **life** & **bid** thee feed,
> **By** the **stream** & **o'er** the mead;
> **Gave** thee **cloth**ing of de**light**,
> **Soft**est **cloth**ing **wooly bright**;
> **Gave** thee **such** a **ten**der **voice**,
> **Mak**ing **all** the **val**es re**joice**:
> **Lit**tle **Lamb** who **made** thee
> **Dost** thou **know** who **made** thee

The other type of "falling" rhythm is the dactyl which consists of a hard beat followed by two soft ones: DUM-di-di. It is not a common metre but you can see a "falling" dactylic rhythm emerging in some poems. William Blake's *Holy Thursday* from the *Songs of Innocence* shows a dactylic rhythm in places but it also exemplifies some of the problems which can happen with metrical analysis. Let's look at the first verse:

> **Twas** on a **Ho**ly **Thurs**day their **inn**ocent **fac**es **clean**
> The **chil**dren **walk**ing **two** & **two** in **red** & **blue** & **green**
> **Grey** headed **bead**les **walk**d before with **wands** as **white** as **snow**
> **Till** into the **high** dome of **Pauls** they like **Thames** waters **flow**

If you look at the first line, you can see that it begins with a dactyl (**Twas** on a) followed by a trochee (**Hol**y) but then a strange thing happens in the line, there is, if you read it carefully, a distinct pause or what is known as a "caesura" – a break in the line – and the rhythm becomes a rising one after this: there's an iamb followed by an anapest and an iamb:

their **inn**ocent **fac**es **clean** (iamb, anapest, iamb)

This line shows the problems with metrical analysis; if you're not careful you can really get tied up into knots! But this said, you can use it to analyse poetry in an interesting way because if you look back at that opening line of Blake's poem you can see that the poet has a falling rhythm on his announcement of the day of "Holy Thursday", but a rising rhythm when describing the children; you could argue there's a mournful rhythm on his proclamation of the day, but a positive one when describing the children, which exactly chimes with the message of the poem which appears to argue that it is the human spirit and not human rituals which create meaning in life.

Use these descriptions to help you describe the effect of the rhythm:

Fast: speedy; fast-paced; quick; lively; energetic; enthusiastic; passionate; fiery;

Slow; sluggish; heavy; slow-paced; emphatic; leaden; lethargic; tired; lugubrious; gloomy.

Next step: read Furniss and Bath, *Reading Poetry*, chapter 12.

Using acronyms to prompt thoughts

A good way of making sure that you are detailed in your analysis of language is to devise your own acronym to help you cover the points that your course expects you to. This is one possible acronym:

FREE 5 TIGERS

Each letter represent a type of analysis:

> **F**igure it out -- use your intuition, always THINK!
> **R**hyme – look for the way a poem rhymes and why it rhymes that way.
> **E**vidence -- everything has to be backed up with evidence/quotation.
> **E**xplanation – explain what is happening in a quote.
> **5** Ws – e.g. What is happening? Where is it happening? Who is it happening to? **W**hen did it happen? **W**hy is it

being written about?
Themes – Discuss the ideas and concept that are explored in a text
Imagery – Look at all the poetic devices in a text: the metaphors, similes, personification, onomatopoeia, alliteration
Genre – Look at the type of text, and the conventions of that genre; how does the text both conform and subvert the genre?
Evaluation – How effective is the text and why?
Rhythm – Analyse the rhythmic effects in the language.
Structure – Analyse the structure of the text and think about how its form and structure shape meanings in a text.

Next step: This crib sheet from the university of Texas is useful: http://uwc.utexas.edu/handouts/poetry-analysis/
Read *Reading Poetry* by Furniss and Bath. Think of your own acronym to help you analyse the poems.

Key concepts

Blake's *Songs of Innocence and Experience* is jam-packed with his exploration of his favourite themes: innocence and experience. It is worth thinking about these concepts again and again, considering what the poems are telling you about these important ideas. However, just as important is for you to think for yourself about what you think of these themes. This section will help you do that.

What is "innocence" in your view? Do you think you're still "innocent"? Who do you know who is "innocent"? What animals, things and places symbolize innocence in your view? Why? Why are they innocent in your view? When were you innocent? What people do you associate with innocence?

Here are some thoughts:
Innocence is believing everyone is good

Innocence involves being ignorant about sex, murder, death, unfairness

In the Garden of Eden, Adam and Eve were innocent before they ate from the tree of knowledge

In Paradise, people are innocent

Young children are innocent

Innocence is not knowing about culture

Innocence is living in the moment

What do you think? It's important that you think carefully about what you think innocence is.

Experience

What is "experience"? What are you "experienced" in? Who do you know who is "experienced"?

Here are some thoughts about what you might think constitutes "experience" or is connected with it:

Growing up

Putting on an act

Being self-conscious

Deceit

Sex

Puberty

Learning about cruelty

What do you think? I think it's worth taking the time to write an extended piece of writing about experience and innocence and what you think these words actually mean in real life. This could be a series of poems, a short story or just a reflective piece of writing. Or equally you could write about what innocence and experience together, comparing and contrasting them. Can innocence exist as a concept without the idea of experience? Does the mere fact that you are writing about innocence mean that you're "experienced"?

Blake on the internet

There is a mass of material about William Blake on the internet.

The Blake society has a links page to many important links, though not all of them are working at the time of writing this: http://www.blakesociety.org/about-blake/blakes-works-2/

The British Museum has a number of important works and articles in its archive: http://www.britishmuseum.org/explore/highlights/articles/w/william_blake_1757-1827.aspx

The complete works and prose can be found here: http://www.blakearchive.org/blake/erdman.html

Blake at the Tate contains good links to his art: http://www.tate.org.uk/art/artists/william-blake-39

The William Blake Archive is astonishing: http://www.blakearchive.org/blake/

The Complete Works including the art can be found here: http://www.william-blake.org/

The Blake concordance: find genuine transcripts of the poems here: http://www.concordancesoftware.co.uk/webconcordances/blake/framconc.htm

Academic analysis: http://eview.anu.edu.au/cross-sections/vol1/pdf/ch12.pdf

Study Guides: Gradesaver is quite reductive in that it offers its points as definite answers rather opinions: http://www.gradesaver.com/songs-of-innocence-and-of-experience/study-guide/about/

Spark Notes is again reductive but worth a look: http://www.sparknotes.com/poetry/blake/

Sagar is a bit better, but a little negative about the poetry: http://www.keithsagar.co.uk/Blake/index.html

Blake's notebooks. These are fascinating and show how careful Blake's working processes were: http://www.bl.uk/onlinegallery/ttp/blake/accessible/introduction.html

Blake and comics can be found here:
http://www.english.ufl.edu/imagetext/archives/v3_2/

You can find the beginning of David Erdman's *Prophet Against Empire*, a seminal book about Blake here:
http://books.google.co.uk/books?id=iotEKFEbXRAC&printsec=frontcover&dq=isbn:0486267199&hl=en&sa=X&ei=HmX9UZr4KsaNOIrdgKgL&redir_esc=y#v=onepage&q&f=false

This blog devoted to Northrop Frye, a very important Blake critic, contains some interesting stuff:
http://fryeblog.blog.lib.mcmaster.ca/category/blake/

This Allan Ginsberg website contains some interesting thoughts on Blake, who influenced the world's most famous Beat poet:
http://ginsbergblog.blogspot.co.uk/2011/11/william-blakes-birthday.html

My own websites have aimed to bring together what material I can, as well posting many of my lessons and students' responses to the poems:
   http://williamblakereloaded.wordpress.com and
http://williamblakepoetry.blogspot.co.uk/

The Bible

Why do you need to know about the Bible to be a good English Literature student? Why do you need to know about it if you are studying Blake? Surely, it's a religious text not a literary one? Well, yes, it is, but it is also possibly the most influential literary text ever written. Until comparatively recently, the Bible influenced every English writer because it was the main text most people listened to and read since most writers had Christian upbringings. This is particularly true of Blake, who was steeped in the Bible, and refers to its stories, imagery and ideas in many of his poems.

The Bible is divided into two sections: The Old Testament and The New Testament. The Old Testament forms the Torah for the Jewish religion, but also the first part of the Christian Bible. It is a collection of stories, the first of which was possibly written down in 3500 BC and drawn together by religious scholars over the ages. For the purposes of the English Literature student, the most important edition of the Bible is the King James Version or Authorised King James' Version (AKJV) or (KJB) published in 1611. This English translation of the Bible is widely considered to be the most beautiful and is certainly the most influential; phrases it uses are often quoted in much succeeding literature. You can find it online here: http://www.kingjamesbibleonline.org/1611-Bible/

A more comprehensible version is the New International Version (NIV), which lacks the poetry of the AKJV but is easier to understand.

Genesis: the Creation of Earth

In a nutshell: God makes the universe, earth, animals and humans in seven days.

Key quote, Genesis, chapter 1, verse 1 (AKJV): "In the beginning God created the heavens and the earth. Now the earth was formless and empty, darkness was over the surface of the deep, and the Spirit of God was hovering over the waters."

Influences: we see references to this poems by Blake such as

Songs of Innocence and Experience: A Study Guide

Introduction to Experience and *Earth's Answer*.

Genesis: the story of the Garden of Eden

In a nutshell: God creates Adam, the first man, and then Eve, from Adam's rib, as a mate for Adam. He allows Adam and Eve to roam freely in Eden -- the paradise he has created -- but forbids them to eat from the tree of knowledge. Eve is persuaded by the serpent (the devil or Satan) to eat the fruit from the tree of knowledge by saying that she will become as knowledgeable as God. Eve eats the apple and then persuades Adam to eat it too so that they are equal. God sees that they are covering up their nakedness and that they are ashamed. He knows that they've eaten from the tree. He punishes them by ordering that men will have to work very hard to have enough to eat, women will always suffer in childbirth and humans will die. He makes the serpent crawl on its belly.

Key quote: Genesis, chapter 3, verse 16: "To the woman God said, 'I will make your pains in childbearing very severe; with painful labour you will give birth to children. Your desire will be for your husband, and he will rule over you.'"

Influences: this is one of the most influential stories ever written and is constantly referenced in poetry, plays and novels. St Augustine interpreted this story as meaning that everyone born after Adam and Eve is born into sin because their sin has been passed on to all their descendants. He called this "original sin": this is a very important idea in Christianity and many Christians still believe in it as a concept. However, non-conformist Christian writers like Blake rejected the idea as being deeply oppressive. Look for references to "forbidden fruit", paradise, original sin.

Noah and the Flood

In a nutshell: God is angry with mankind and kills them all with a flood, except for Noah who he tells to make a boat and put his family and all the animals on it.

Key quote: Genesis, chapter 7, verse 6 (AKJV): "Noah was six hundred years old when the floodwaters came on the earth. And Noah and his sons and his wife and his sons' wives entered the ark to escape the waters of the flood. Pairs of clean and unclean animals, of birds and of all creatures that move along the ground, male and female, came to Noah and entered the ark, as God had commanded Noah."

Influences: The idea of "Armageddon", of escaping from danger, of preserving life is central to countless texts, particularly Blake's poems such as *London* and *The Tyger*.

The Tower of Babel

In a nutshell: The people of earth speak one language and build a huge tower, the tower of Babel, which reaches to the heavens to show how powerful they are. God, annoyed that they are trying to be like him, destroys the tower and makes everyone speak a different language so that they don't understand each other.

Key quote: Genesis, chapter 11, verse 6(AKJV): The LORD said, "If as one people speaking the same language they have begun to do this, then nothing they plan to do will be impossible for them. Come, let us go down and confuse their language so they will not understand each other."

Influences: the idea of language confusing and deceiving people is central to many Blake poems such as *The Human Abstract*, *The Garden of Love*, and *The Voice of the Ancient Bard*.

Abraham & Isaac

In a nutshell: God gives Abraham a covenant (a holy promise) and tells him that the Jewish people will become slaves of another people, but then will be rescued by God. Abraham is told to sacrifice his son, Isaac, to prove his obedience to God; Abraham gets his son ready to kill him, but suddenly a heifer or goat appears and God tells him that he can sacrifice that instead; Abraham's son is saved because Abraham had proved his worth.

Influences: the idea of doing your duty even though it harms you and your family is a central theme of many texts. You could argue that many of Blake's poems explore the central conundrum of the Abraham & Isaac story: how should fathers treat their children?

Joseph and his brothers

In a nutshell: Joseph was a favourite son of Jacob and was given a lovely, multi-coloured coat by Jacob. Joseph has strange dreams about the corn and the stars bowing down to him. When he tells his brothers about these, they are jealous, and are jealous of his coat. The brothers plot to kill him but are persuaded by the eldest brother Reuben to throw him into a pit. Then some merchants come by and the brothers take Joseph's coat and sell him to the merchants. He was taken to Egypt, fell out with the merchant and was imprisoned. But news came to the Pharaoh of Joseph and his strange dreams. Joseph tells his dreams to the Pharaoh which warn of famine and tells him to store grain so that the country is prepared. Joseph becomes a Governor because the Pharaoh is so pleased with him. Meanwhile, his brothers are starving in Canaan. Joseph realises they have changed and rescues them, bringing them to live with him in Egypt.

Influences: apart from spawning a musical, this story has been re-interpreted many times. The central motif of the abject slave becoming very powerful, ascending from the bottom of the social ladder to the top is common in many stories. The power of dreams is central to many Blake poems such as *A Dream*, *The Angel* etc.

Sodom and Gomorrah

In a nutshell: people were behaving very badly in Sodom and Gomorrah, having sex with people they supposedly shouldn't have sex with, possibly having homosexual sex so God destroyed the city and killed all the inhabitants with fire and brimstone.

Influences: these names are still synonymous with concepts of sexual depravity and frequently referenced when talking about issues connected with sex and corruption.

Moses in "Exodus" the next book in the Bible after Genesis

In a nutshell: Moses hears God speaking from a burning bush saying that he will rescue the Jewish people from slavery in Egypt. Moses leads the Jewish people out of Egypt, known as the Exodus (listen to the Bob Marley song) to the promised land, Israel – which is the name of God, who is also known as Elohim and Jahweh, his name though is spelt out fully in Jewish literature. Called by God to Mount Sinai, God gives Moses the Ten Commandments, vital rules that must be obeyed.

Key quote: Exodus 20:1-17 (AKJV): "And God spake all these words, saying, I *am* the LORD thy God, which have brought thee out of the land of Egypt, out of the house of bondage. Thou shalt have no other gods before me. Thou shalt not make unto thee any graven image, or any likeness *of anything* that *is* in heaven above, or that *is* in the earth beneath, or that *is* in the water under the earth: thou shalt not bow down thyself to them, nor serve them: for I the LORD thy God *am* a jealous God, visiting the iniquity of the fathers upon the children unto the third and fourth *generation* of them that hate me; and shewing mercy unto thousands of them that love me, and keep my commandments."

Influences: much literature explores the consequences of rules and regulations. Blake's poems such as *The Garden of Love* are particularly relevant.

Samson and Delilah

In a nutshell: For forty years the Israelis suffered at the hands of the Philistines, a terrible enemy who lived near the sea. However, a mighty warrior Samson was born who not only could kill lions, but also Philistines. Samson fell in love with a beautiful woman called Delilah who was secretly working for the Philistines; she discovers the secret to his strength is his long hair. When he was asleep, she signaled to the Philistines to cut off his hair; Samson was captured and blinded, and taken to Gaza where he was thrown in prison. The Philistines celebrated their triumph in their temple and brought out the blinded prisoner to highlight their victory; he was put between the pillars of a doorway so that everyone could see him. The crowd jeered at how weak he was. Asking the Lord for help, Samson pushed the pillars on either side of him over making the temple collapse, killing everyone inside, including himself.

Influences: a tremendously influential story. Delilah is the original "femme fatale"; the woman who leads a great man to his doom. The story of the injured, weakened warrior who has one last victory has influenced numerous stories from King Arthur to James Bond. In Blake, the Bard is a "Samson-like" figure; someone who is defeated but has hidden power.

David and Goliath

In a nutshell: Weedy but clever David defeats Goliath in a fight by being clever and using a sling-shot to hit him with stones. David becomes King and marries Bathsheba after making her pregnant and causing her husband's death by sending him to fight in a battle.

Influences: hardly a day goes by when this story isn't referenced in one or another. It is an archetypal story in that it shows how brains beat brawn. Blake explores the consequences of deceitful cunning in many poems such as *A Poison Tree*.

King Solomon's wisdom

In a nutshell: The son of David, King Solomon was asked by God in a dream what he most wanted and he replied "wisdom". One day, two mothers came to him claiming that a baby was theirs and asked Solomon to decide who was the real mother. Solomon got out his sword and said he would cut the baby in two and give them half each. One of the women said this was a good idea, while the other broke down in tears and said that she would rather the other woman had the baby than see the child killed. Solomon then knew she was the mother. After this story, people realized he had the wisdom of God.

Influences: the idea of the wise ruler or the wise man appears in many stories such as Prospero in Shakespeare's *The Tempest* to Thomas Cromwell in Hilary Mantel's *Wolf Hall*. Blake had real contempt for rigid law-givers, but believed that people should decide what is good and bad for themselves.

The New Testament -- The Gospels

In a nutshell: These four books were written by Mark, Luke, Matthew and John. They are all about the life of Jesus and contain similar stories about him, but sometimes vary in their details.

Key ideas: the **Annunciation**. An angel announces to Mary that God will impregnate her and give her a baby who is the son of God. Mary stays a virgin. The **Nativity**: Jesus is born in a manger because King Herod is looking to kill him, because it has been prophecized that he will be king of Jews. Jesus is the son of a carpenter, Joseph and Mary. He is born in Bethlehem. He is visited as a baby by three shepherds, three wise men and three kings. Little is written about his growing up in the Gospels. When he is a young man, John the Baptist begins talking about the coming of the Lord and baptising people to get them ready. He sees Jesus and calls him a "Lamb", the son of God. Jesus goes into the desert and wrestles with the Devil for forty days and nights. He wins and comes back and starts preaching to people about the coming Kingdom of Heaven. He feeds 5000 people with a loaf of bread; he walks on water; he calms the water while on a fishing boat in a storm; he raises Lazarus from the dead. He has twelve disciples, or followers, including Judas and Peter. He communicates his message in "parables": interesting stories with a message. Famous ones are:

The Prodigal Son: there's a good son and a bad son. The bad son spends all the money his Dad has given him on wine, gambling and women. Comes back and has to sleep in father's pig pen to survive. Too ashamed to show his face. His brother finds him and is disgusted. His father sees him and is delighted, announcing there is to be a party about his return and that they should "kill the fatted calf" (the most expensive animal) for the meal. This was Blake's favourite parable because it is all about forgiveness and love.

The house built on sand. There are two houses: one built on firm land. One built on sand. The one on sand is built quickly and looks great. But falls down in a storm. The other one stays up.

The Good Samaritan. A traveller gets beaten up by bandits but is not helped by his fellow men, and instead is rescued from death by a foreigner, a Samaritan.

Jesus gives a "Sermon on the Mount" when he gives a series of famous sayings called the Beatitudes, which are very important and often quoted:

The Beatitudes. Matthew Chapters 5-7 (AKJV): "And seeing the multitudes, he went up into a mountain: and when he was set, his disciples came unto him: and he opened his mouth, and taught them, saying, Blessed are the poor in spirit: for theirs is the kingdom of heaven. Blessed are they that mourn: for they shall be comforted. Blessed are the meek: for they shall inherit the earth. Blessed are they which do hunger and thirst after righteousness: for they shall be filled. Blessed are the merciful: for they shall obtain mercy. Blessed are the pure in heart: for they shall see God. Blessed are the peacemakers: for they shall be called the children of God. Blessed are they which are persecuted for righteousness' sake: for theirs is the kingdom of heaven. Blessed are ye, when men shall revile you, and persecute you, and shall say all manner of evil against you falsely, for my sake."

Jesus is "transfigured". Matthew 17 (AKJV): "And after six days Jesus taketh Peter, James, and John his brother, and bringeth them up into an high mountain apart, and was transfigured before them: and his face did shine as the sun, and his raiment was white as the light. And, behold, there appeared unto them Moses and Elijah talking with him."

Jesus goes into Jerusalem, the holy city, to announce he is the son of God on a donkey (a very lowly animal). He knows he is going to die. He holds a "Last Supper" where bread is broken and wine drunk. He says the bread is his flesh and the wine is his blood. He tells Peter that he will betray him three times before the cock crows.

Betrayal: He is betrayed in the garden of Gethsemane by Judas who kisses him to show the Romans who want to arrest him that he is Jesus. His disciples are asked if they know him. Peter denies knowing him three times before the cock crows.

He is put on trial by Pontius Pilate who washes his hands to indicate he doesn't know what to do with him. The Jewish Pharisees, annoyed by the way Jesus has criticised them, ask for him to be crucify instead one of their men. He is crucified and dies on the Cross. A few days after he is put in his tomb, he is discovered preaching by his disciples. This is the resurrection.

The Ascension: Acts Chapter 1, verses 9-11 (AKJV) Later, Jesus ascends back to heaven: "And when he had spoken these things, while they beheld, he was taken up; and a cloud received him out of their sight. And while they looked stedfastly toward heaven as he went up, behold, two men stood by them in white apparel; which also said, Ye men of Galilee, why stand ye gazing up into heaven? this same Jesus, which is taken up from you into heaven, shall so come in like manner as ye have seen him go into heaven. There is a promise though that there will be a "second coming" when Jesus will return to earth to separate the saved and the damned on Judgment Day.

Influences: Blake was massively influenced by the figure of Jesus.

The rest of the New Testament

In a nutshell: In Acts, we learn about the story of Paul (formerly Saul) who was a tax collector but on the road to Damascus was converted into believing in Jesus and God. This the story:

Acts 9:1-20 Authorized (AKJV): "And Saul, yet breathing out threatenings and slaughter against the disciples of the Lord, went unto the high priest, and desired of him letters to Damascus to the synagogues, that if he found any of this way, whether they were men or women, he might bring them bound unto Jerusalem. And as he journeyed, he came near Damascus: and suddenly there shined round about him a light from heaven: and he fell to the earth, and heard a voice saying unto him, Saul, Saul, why persecutest thou me? And he said, Who art thou, Lord? And the Lord said, I am Jesus whom thou persecutest: *it is* hard for thee to kick against the pricks. And he trembling and astonished said,

Lord, what wilt thou have me to do? And the Lord *said* unto him, Arise, and go into the city, and it shall be told thee what thou must do. And the men which journeyed with him stood speechless, hearing a voice, but seeing no man. And Saul arose from the earth; and when his eyes were opened, he saw no man: but they led him by the hand, and brought *him* into Damascus. And he was three days without sight, and neither did eat nor drink."

He goes on to establish the Christian church but is imprisoned by the Romans for his religious beliefs. In prison, Paul writes a number of letters giving advice to Christians who are setting up the church; Paul invents much the structure of the church.

Book 1 of Corinthians 13, (NIV): This is the most famous lines he wrote: "When I was a child, I talked like a child, I thought like a child, I reasoned like a child. When I became a man, I put the ways of childhood behind me. For now we see only a reflection as in a mirror; then we shall see face to face. Now I know in part; then I shall know fully, even as I am fully known."

The King James Bible (AKJV) is much more poetic but more difficult to understand: "When I was a child, I spake as a child, I understood as a child, I thought as a child: but when I became a man, I put away childish things. For now we see through a glass, darkly; but then face to face: now I know in part; but then shall I know even as also I am known. And now abideth faith, hope, charity, these three; but the greatest of these *is* charity."

Revelations

In a nutshell: this is the last book in the New Testament and by far the strangest. Many people have divined "occult" meanings from it. It prophecies the end of the earth and the second coming of Christ, Judgment Day.

Revelation Chapter 6, vs 1-2, New International Version: "I watched as the Lamb opened the first of the seven seals. Then I heard one of the four living creatures say in a voice like thunder, "Come and see!" I looked, and there before me was a white horse! Its rider held a bow, and he was given a crown, and he rode out as a conqueror bent on conquest."

The Lamb is Jesus Christ who opens the book from which four horsemen come out: a white horse which symbolises Conquest, a red horse which symbolises War, a black horse which symbolises Famine, and a pale horse which symbolises Death.

Revelation Chapter 6, verses 7-8 (NIV): "When the Lamb opened the fourth seal, I heard the voice of the fourth living creature say, "Come and see!" I looked and there before me was a pale horse! Its rider was named Death, and Hell was following close behind him. They were given power over a fourth of the earth to kill by sword, famine, and plague, and by the wild beasts of the earth."

Influences: Dante's *Divine Comedy* which is about the poet's journey to Hell, Puragatory and Heaven is based on *Revelations*. This was a book Blake returns to again and again in his poetry. He clearly loved its apocalyptic atmosphere.

Babylon and the Whore of Babylon

In *Revelations* a woman, who is a prostitute or harlot, is to blame for the "fallen" state of mankind. **Chapter 17, verse 5** (AKJV): "And upon her forehead was a name written a mystery: Babylon The Great, the mother of harlots and abominations of the Earth.... And I saw the woman drunken with the blood of the saints, and with the blood of the martyrs of Jesus: and when I saw her, I wondered with great admiration."

Next step: The Brick Testament is a lot of fun; it's a sort of Lego version of the Bible. Although it's devised for kids, it's a great way of learning the stories. http://thebrickbible.com/

If I am really honest, I have to say that I have found the *The DK Children's Illustrated Bible* (1994) by Selina Hastings the most useful to dip in and out because it presents the stories so attractively and provides some useful contextual points as well.

http://www.dk.co.uk/nf/Book/BookDisplay/0,,9781409364511,00.html

Influences: all of Shakespeare's plays are full of Biblical references, John Milton's *Paradise Lost* is based on Genesis, and most classical and romantic poetry is shot through with Biblical imagery and themes. Blake's *London* is clearly influenced by the book with the "youthful harlot" bringing havoc to babies, wives and marriage in the final verse.

Title pages

These are worth looking at even if you are not commenting upon Blake's art. There are three introductory pages. The first tells us the book is the *Songs of Innocence and Experience*; the second is a picture of the Piper in the *Introduction to Innocence* and the third is another title page, *Songs of Innocence*. The first page tells us that the books are "Showing the Two Contrary States of the Human Soul". These three illuminated title pages above all show Blake's ambitions: he is aiming to describe human experience with these poems, he is going to take us to places we haven't thought about and he wants to show that there are two distinct sides to the "Human Soul": innocence and experience. He is giving us a new language, which is both pictorial and linguistic, to describe human experience. The title pages announce his enormous ambition.

Questions

Why does Blake have three title pages?

What do the illustrations tell us about his themes and imagery?

What do you think of the pictures?

Francis Gilbert

Introduction (Innocence)

Pre-reading

What are the best introductions to films/books/music you have come across? How important is a good introduction?

>Piping down the valleys wild
>Piping songs of pleasant glee
>　On a cloud I saw a child.
>　And he laughing said to me.
>
>Pipe a song about a Lamb:
>So I piped with merry chear,
>Piper pipe that song again --
>So I piped, he wept to hear.
>
>Drop thy pipe thy happy pipe
>Sing thy songs of happy chear,
>　So I sung the same again
>While he wept with joy to hear.
>
>Piper sit thee down and write
>In a book that all may read --
>So he vanish'd from my sight,
>And I pluck'd a hollow reed.
>
>　And I made a rural pen,
>　And I stain'd the water clear,
>　And I wrote my happy songs
>　Every child may joy to hear

Questions

Where has the Piper come from?

　Who is the "child on the cloud" do you think? What does he/she symbolize?

　Why does the child ask the Piper to sing the song and then

write them down?
What is the effect of the rhyme and rhythm in this poem?

Creative response
Write your own introduction to a set of poems/reflections about innocence, either as a short description or a poem.

Analysis
You can see me explain this poem here on YouTube:
http://www.youtube.com/watch?v=md8J1C9rppA

What effects are created when the poem is sung or read aloud?

I worked for a long time on a sung version of this song and decided to sing it in a very "non-traditional" way, giving it a modern beat, and singing it in a half-spoken, sinister fashion. You can watch and listen to it here on YouTube:

http://www.youtube.com/watch?v=p4xNrWPFCOg

I'm sure lots of people will hate it, but some might find the interpretation thought-provoking because I sing the song very much against type. It appears, on the surface, to be a happy song about a piper piping a song – and then singing it – to a child on a cloud. Other sung versions and readings of the song emphasize the happiness of the poem. When you read out aloud you can really hear and feel the effect of the alliteration and repetition; the repetition of "piping" and "pipe" creates a bouncing, very rhythmic effect, while the alliteration of the powerful consonantal "p" sound creates a punchy drive to the poem. You can also hear the effect of the vowel sounds when you read it: the long vowel sound of the "i" in "pipe" generates, for me, quite a sharp singing, slightly "spacey" tone to the poem, giving it what you might call an "ethereal" quality. Like many of his poems, the text has the quality of a hallucination; it is, after all, about a musician playing and then singing to a child on a cloud, presumably an angel. The simple rhyming quatrains blaze out when you read it; you always hear the rhymes making the words chime together. The punctuation is important; it's very important to note Blake's punctuation which shows where he felt the pauses should go. For example, there is a full stop at the end of the third line which makes you realize that

Blake wants you to think about the vision of the child; the pause is there possibly to convey the piper's astonishment at seeing the child on the cloud.

What questions do you have about the poem?

I have so many questions still about this poem but here are a few:

Who is the child on a cloud?

Why does the child weep when he hears the song?

Why does the child/angel want the piper to write down his songs?

What interests you most about the poem? Why?

For me, I'm most interested in the two characters in the poem; the piper/poet and the child on the cloud, and their relationship. What was the piper doing in the "valleys wild"? What kind of person is he? Why does the child feel that the poems should be written down? It feels like the pair of them are aiming to spread the word about the songs of "happy chear"; the child wants to generate a new culture, a new world of song and "happy chear". Why? Is it because the world is so miserable?

What is the poem about?

At its most basic level, this is a story about a piper who meets a child on a cloud who first asks the piper to pipe a song about a "Lamb" for him, and then sing it. After hearing the song played on the pipe and then played again, the child weeps – clearly from happiness. Then the child asks the piper to sing the song, and finally to write it down, which the piper does with a "hollow reed".

Apparently, the child is an angel of some sort and the Lamb he asks the Piper to sing about is Jesus Christ; the Lamb was, and is, a very common image for Jesus. So you could say that the Piper by writing songs about Jesus is spreading the Word of God. But equally, the Lamb could be a "natural" Lamb and the piper, who has come from the "valleys wild", is actually spreading the word about the marvels of nature. This was a common idea at this time as well.

What effects does the language create?

The language is deceptively simple and repetitious; but I found you need to read the poem a few times to work out exactly what is going on. Blake plays around with nouns and verbs in an interesting fashion; there are the nouns of the "piper" and the "pipe" and the verbal phrases of "piping" and "piped".

For me, this creates a great sense of musicality and playfulness; there is almost the quality of a tongue-twister about the poem. The syntax is sometimes, though not always, shaped by the demands of the rhyme scheme and the ballad form. For example, Blake writes "On a cloud I saw a child" rather than "I saw a child on a cloud" – which would have sounded more natural. The effect of this word order is to emphasize the ethereal quality of the poem, to make us see more vividly the cloud and then the child on it.

What are the effects of the poem's structure and form?

Nicholas Marsh points out that nearly the whole song has a "trochaic" rhythm (Marsh: p. 12) The form is that of a ballad; a sung story, which were traditionally structured in quatrains – four line verses which have alternate rhymes.

What are the similarities and differences between other texts?

The most obvious point of comparison is the *Introduction* to the *Songs of Experience*, which is very different. In that poem, the Bard is asked to rescue mankind and the earth from destruction and desolation. However both poems are "invocations"; that is they involve characters being "called" to do things. In this *Introduction*, the piper is "called" by the angel child to play, sing and write down his songs for the children. In the other poem, the Bard, or poet, is called by the Holy Word – or God -- to rescue the world from destruction. The Bard is very similar to the Piper in that he is a poet and singer, while the child on a cloud is similar to the Holy Word of God. So while the poems' imagery and tone are very different, they do share these striking similarities.

How do other people interpret this poem? Find sources/links…

Some critics like Keynes read the poem as an allegory which is about the transition from an oral culture to a written one; the Piper begins the poem by playing a tune, which is wordless, and then, at the bidding of the child, turning it into a verbal song, and then finally writing it down. Thus we see the movement from a non-verbal culture (the tune) to a verbal, spoken culture (the song) to finally a written culture (the written poem). There is embedded within this happy song a sense of loss: the water is "stained" by the ink of the pen, indicating a sense of pollution. Equally, the song is written down so that every child might hear it, something which couldn't happen without printing technology; the Piper couldn't physically travel to every child singing his song. So while there may be a sense of loss with the writing down of the poem, there is also a new sense of equality; "every" child is now going to have contact with the song.

What might make a good creative response to the poem?

Write a poem/story about a rock/pop/hip-hop star like 50 cent who is called by a ghost/angel/God/anyone to write songs for children.

How might you teach this poem?

Doing a "fill-in-the-blanks" exercise where you blank out the key nouns and verbs can work very successfully with this poem because it gets students thinking about Blake's lexical choices and discussing why he repeated certain words, or used certain images:

> Piping down the valleys wild
> ------ songs of pleasant glee
> On a cloud I saw a ----.
> And he laughing said to me.
>
> Pipe a song about a ----:
> So I piped with merry chear,
> Piper pipe that song again --
> So I piped, he wept to hear.
>
> Drop thy pipe thy happy pipe
> Sing thy songs of happy ----,
> So I sung the same again

While he --- with joy to hear.

---- sit thee down and write
In a book that all may read --
So he vanish'd from my sight,
And I pluck'd a hollow reed.

And I made a rural ---,
And I ---- the water clear,
And I wrote my happy songs
Every child may --- to hear

Have a go at doing this exercise with other poems too: it will really help you think about Blake's use of language.

The Shepherd

Pre-reading

Who are the people in your life who have looked after you? How might you describe them?

How sweet is the Shepherds sweet lot,
From the morn to the evening he strays:
He shall follow his sheep all the day
And his tongue shall be filled with praise.

For he hears the lambs innocent call.
And he hears the ewes tender reply.
He is watchful while they are in peace,
For they know when their Shepherd is nigh

Questions

Why is the Shepherd's lot "sweet"?
   What does he do all day?
   Why is his tongue filled with praise, do you think?
   Why is the Shepherd watchful?

Who does the Shepherd represent?

Creative response

Write a poem/description/story about a caring person who looks after people in some sort of way. Use imagery to describe him or her.

Analysis

You can watch me explain this poem on YouTube here: http://www.youtube.com/watch?v=baBzJd6t97M

MEANING: What is the poem about?

Keynes says this poem is "a simple one and needs little comment" (p. 133) but a close examination of the poem suggests it is more complex than it first appears. Ostensibly, it is about "the Shepherd": the definite article "the" is important, he's not "a" (indefinite article) shepherd. The use of the definite article suggests the importance and uniqueness of the shepherd. Blake uses the adjective "sweet" to describe the "lot" or fate/lifestyle of the shepherd. He "strays" from the "morn to the evening"; this verb has connotations of a careful, joyful, wandering existence. And yet, there is a tension because he "follows his sheep all the day"; so he is both free in the sense that he "strays" but also inextricably linked to his sheep. There is a sense here that because he loves his sheep -- because he loves following them -- it isn't a loss of freedom. Indeed, his "tongue" is "filled with praise": he is positive about the world and his flock. He has made a conscious effort to say "yes" to the world. Above all, the Shepherd is a "listener" and an "observer"; he "hears" the lamb and watches while his sheep sleep. He takes joy in seeing the loving relationships that shape his flock. The poem shifts perspective in the last line because we learn that the sheep "know when their Shepherd is nigh"; they are aware that he is always near.

CONTEXTS: What possibly influenced the writing of the poem? How we might read the poem now? The poem evokes what Keynes calls "Arcadian peace and trustfulness"; it shows what paradise is like on earth. This is particularly true of the illustration that accompanies the poem. Images of the Garden of Eden are important here; this is Blake building up a picture of what paradise might look like on earth. The poem also has "Biblical echoes"; the figure of the Shepherd is important in the Bible. In *the Gospel According To John*, Chapter 10, verse 14, Jesus says: "I am the good shepherd, and know my [sheep], and am known of mine." There is a sense that the shepherd in Blake's poem is Jesus and the sheep are humankind. This line from Psalms (A Psalm of David), Chapter 23, verses 1-6 is relevant too: "The LORD [is] my shepherd; I shall not want." Notice how the Shepherd is an "intimate" God who is benignly watching over people. Blake's re-interpretation of Christianity is possibly more relevant to us now than it was when he was alive; throughout the poems he is arguing for a "human" God, a God who listens and cares, rather than one who is distant and judges.

TECNIQUES and EFFECTS: What linguistic and poetic devices does the poem use and what are their effects? The apparent simplicity of structure belies real sophistication with rhythm and rhyme. The rhythm of the poem is particularly interesting; there is a "bouncing" rhythm to the poem which deploys three main beats with great skill and variety. The syllables highlighted in bold are where I believe the main stresses are:

> How **sweet** is the **Shep**herds sweet **lot**,
> From the **morn** to the **eve**ning he **strays**:
> He shall **foll**ow his **sheep** all the **day**
> And his **tongue** shall be **filled** with **praise**.

There is a "rising rhythm" here which conveys hope, pace and joy. Let's look at the first line: we have an "iamb" (a soft stress followed by a heavy stress, di-DUM) followed by two anapests (two soft stresses followed by a heavy stress, di-di-DUM). The varying of rhythm, the mixture of the iamb and the anapests, gives the poem a real spring in its step. While the poem is mostly composed of sprightly anapests, it does change in places to using iambs, such as the last two syllables, which emphasize both through the use of rhyme and rhythm the positivity of the shepherd. The use of adjectives are important in the poem: Blake repeats "sweet" to convey the beauty of the Shepherd's life, while he talks about the lamb's "innocent" call, and the ewe's "tender" reply. Through the use of adjectives Blake is portraying a picture of what the ideal relationship between parent and child might be: it should be a caring, listening relationship where children are allowed and afforded the room for their innocence.

Further investigations

Blake created a number of different versions of the poem, which you can compare here on the Blake archive: http://www.blakearchive.org/exist/blake/archive/comparison.xq?selection=compare&copies=all&bentleynum=B5&copyid=songsie.b&java=. You should also read the Biblical references in the poem, noted above.

The Ecchoing Green

Pre-reading

What are the happiest places you have known in your life? What made them so special? Think in detail about these happy days, describe them in depth, brainstorming your ideas if necessary.

> The Sun does arise,
> And make happy the skies.
> The merry bells ring,
> To welcome the Spring.
> The sky-lark and thrush,
> The birds of the bush,
> Sing louder around,
> To the bells chearful sound,
> While our sports shall be seen
> On the Ecchoing Green.
>
> Old John with white hair
> Does laugh away care,
> Sitting under the oak,
> Among the old folk.

Songs of Innocence and Experience: A Study Guide

> They laugh at our play,
> And soon they all say,
> Such such were the joys,
> When we all girls & boys,
> In our youth time were seen,
> On the Ecchoing Green.
>
> Till the little ones weary,
> No more can be merry
> The sun does descend,
> And our sports have an end:
> Round the laps of their mothers,
> Many sisters and brothers,
> Like birds in their nest,
> Are ready for rest:
> And sport no more seen,
> On the darkening Green.

Questions

Why are the skies "happy" and the bells "cheerful"?
What do people do on the Ecchoing Green?
How do young and old people get along?
How is this poem structured? Why is it structured in this way?
What makes the Ecchoing Green such a happy place?
Why does Blake describe the Ecchoing Green as "darkening" at the end of the poem?

Creative response

Write your own version of *The Ecchoing Green*, structuring it like Blake, having a morning, afternoon and evening/night-time. Use imagery to describe a beautiful place.

Analysis

You can watch a video of me briefly explaining this poem here on YouTube:

http://www.youtube.com/watch?v=-2hCASwiv6o

This poem, much like *The Shepherd*, is painting a picture of the ideal world, the perfect society. It is structured in three verses which offer a "day in the life" of this rural society: with the first verse focusing upon morning, the second on the afternoon, and the third on evening and night. The imagery of the first verse shows how both the human and the animal worlds seem to be at one; this is an idea which is echoed in Blake's illustrations to the poem – make sure you look carefully at them, the URL for this is below in Further Investigations. The "skylark" and "thrush" sing to the "bells chearful sound"; they accompany the man-made bells. There is a sense that the human and animal kingdoms are at one when celebrating the morning. While bells are often associated with church, we find that the people of the village are not in church but on the "ecchoing green"; they are performing "sports" which means they are doing things they enjoy rather than specifically doing "sports", although we get a picture that there is quite a bit of running around.

The rhyming couplets of the poem and the strong rising rhythm which deploys iambs and anapests help create the happy atmosphere as it works in tandem with the imagery. The second verse focuses upon the elderly who are enjoying seeing the children play. The perspective of the poet here is worth noting; the poet presents himself as one of the young people through his use of the possessive pronoun "our". The old people tell the children about the happy days they had when they were young, emphasizing their happiness through the repetition of "such"; there is a sense of passing time here, and loss as well, but there is happiness residing in the memories of their youthful days. In such a way, we can see Blake trying to build a picture of what a real paradise might look like; there would be an acceptance of the passing of time. This theme is further developed in the next verse when the children have to return to "the laps of their mothers" like "birds in their nest". Again we have a sense of the natural and human world being very closely linked; the homes of the children are like "nests". The rhyme of "nest" and "rest" is simple but evocative, suggestive of the safety and cosiness of home. The poem ends on a darker note, with Blake deploying the adjective "darkening" to describe the green at night-time. Again, we have to acknowledge of the finiteness of time, of the fleetiness of life, but an implicit awareness that paradise is achieved precisely because things are finite; death brings an awareness of the preciousness of life.

Further investigations

You can compare different pictorial versions of the poems here: http://www.blakearchive.org/exist/blake/archive/comparison.xq?selection=compare&copies=all&bentleynum=B6&copyid=songsie.b&java=

and here: http://www.blakearchive.org/exist/blake/archive/comparison.xq?selection=compare&copies=all&bentleynum=B7&copyid=songsie.b&java=. Keynes analyses the symbols in the poem in some depth (p. 133) but perhaps in a somewhat reductive fashion.

The Lamb

Pre-reading

Who are the innocent people/things/places you have encountered in your life? What made them innocent? If you could ask any questions to an animal what would they be?

>Little Lamb who made thee
>Dost thou know who made thee
>Gave thee life & bid thee feed,
>By the stream & o'er the mead;
>Gave thee clothing of delight,
>Softest clothing wooly bright;
>Gave thee such a tender voice,
>Making all the vales rejoice:
>Little Lamb who made thee
>Dost thou know who made thee
>
>Little Lamb I'll tell thee,
>Little Lamb I'll tell thee;
>He is called by thy name,

> For he calls himself a Lamb:
> He is meek & he is mild,
> He became a little child:
> I a child & thou a lamb,
> We are called by his name.
> Little Lamb God bless thee,
> Little Lamb God bless thee.

Questions

What questions does the poet ask of the Lamb and what answers does he receive?

Who is the Lamb?

Why does the poet feel the need to bless the Lamb?

Creative response

Building on your notes you got from the pre-reading exercise, write your own poem about a person/animal/thing/object/place that embodies innocence. Use Blake's structure of question and answer if you can, asking questions about the innocence of the creature/thing/place.

Analysis

You can watch a video of me briefly explaining this poem here on YouTube:

http://www.youtube.com/watch?v=HAX_Adn8smY

This poem is based around a "question and answer" structure. The first verse asks the central question: "who made thee" and the second verse provides the answer. The repetition of the question creates a sense of mystery and wonder. The poem suggests that the innocent lamb, with its "softest clothing wooly bright", doesn't know how innocent and charming it looks and is, nor who created him or her. The lamb is not "self-conscious" or speculative about the world around him or her. The poet brings to bear upon the lamb a new world of questioning; the poet prompts the lamb to ask the question about who created him/her. In other words, the poet is a form of teacher or educator, insisting upon the "lamb" or "child" – which the lamb could symbolize – that he learns about the larger things in life: who made him, who brought him to life, who made him conscious. The lamb clearly doesn't have an answer to the question because the poet answers the question for him; "he is called by thy name,/For he calls himself a Lamb". Many critics have interpreted this as being Jesus who is described as a lamb by John the Baptist: "The next day John seeth Jesus coming unto him, and saith, Behold the Lamb of God, which taketh away the sin of the world." (John: 1:29)

What is important here is that Jesus is called by "thy name" and "became a little child". Jesus is a God who is, at heart, innocent like a child; who isn't tainted by cynicism, by selfishness, by nastiness. The poem shifts in perspective in a mysterious and haunting fashion when Blake writes: "I a child & thou a lamb". The poet has become a child by reflecting upon who made the lamb. In other words, the act of reflecting upon who made the innocent lamb has enabled the poet to enter into a "child-like" state. Thus we can see Blake putting forward the argument that "self-consciousness", that "knowledge" does not destroy innocence but actually creates it; you are only truly innocent when are aware of what "experience" is. This is an argument that Blake develops throughout the poems and is well worth considering.

The poem is brilliantly structured. The rhythm is particularly striking. Blake writes, as he does with many of the poems in *Innocence and Experience*, in "trochees"; that is there is a "falling" rhythm created by the text, with a heavy beat being followed by a soft one:

> **Litt**le **Lamb** who **made** thee
> **Dost** thou **know** who **made** thee
> **Gave** thee **life** & **bid** thee feed,
> **By** the **stream** & **o'er** the mead;
> **Gave** thee **cloth**ing of de**light**,
> **Soft**est **cloth**ing **wool**y **bright**;
> **Gave** thee **such** a **ten**der **voice**,
> **Mak**ing **all** the **val**es re**joice**:
> **Litt**le **Lamb** who **made** thee
> **Dost** thou **know** who **made** thee

There's variety in the rhythm, but the beat is very strident and unusual creating a genuinely haunting beat, which pulsates through the poem. *The Tyger* which is the companion poem to the *Lamb* in *Experience* is written in a similar trochaic rhythm but creates a different effect. There's a thumping, violent beat in the *The Tyger*, while in the Lamb there's more of a tender heart-beat.

Further investigations

Blake created a number of different versions of the poem, which you can compare here:

http://www.blakearchive.org/exist/blake/archive/comparison.xq?selection=compare&copies=all&bentleynum=B8&copyid=songsie.b&java=

What are the similarities and differences between the versions?

The Little Black Boy

Pre-reading

Why do you think racism exists? Why have so many religious people been racist?

> My mother bore me in the southern wild,
> And I am black, but O! my soul is white,
> White as an angel is the English child;
> But I am black as if bereav'd of light.
>
> My mother taught me underneath a tree
> And sitting down before the heat of day,
> She took me on her lap and kissed me,
> And pointing to the east began to say.
>
> Look on the rising sun: there God does live
> And gives his light, and gives his heat away.
> And flowers and trees and beasts and men recieve
> Comfort in morning joy in the noon day.

Songs of Innocence and Experience: A Study Guide

And we are put on earth a little space,
That we may learn to bear the beams of love.
And these black bodies and this sun-burnt face
Is but a cloud, and like a shady grove.

For when our souls have learn'd the heat to bear,
The cloud will vanish we shall hear his voice,
Saying: come out from the grove my love & care,
And round my golden tent like lambs rejoice.

Thus did my mother say and kissed me.
And thus I say to little English boy.
When I from black and he from white cloud free,
And round the tent of God like lambs we joy:

I'll shade him from the heat till he can bear,
To lean in joy upon our fathers knee.
And then I'll stand and stroke his silver hair,
And be like him and he will then love me.

Questions

Why is the black boy distressed in the first verse?

What does the mother say to her son? Why are their black bodies like a "shady grove"?

What does the black boy say to the English boy? Why do you think he is speaking to the English boy?

Creative response

Write your own dramatic monologue in which a character speaks about the problems in his/her life connected with prejudice or racial prejudice.

Analysis

You can watch a video of me briefly explaining this poem here on YouTube:

http://www.youtube.com/watch?v=XUrw-FP7IxM

There's much controversy over this poem and what its possible meanings are. But the context of the poem is important; when

Blake wrote it, the British empire was still using the slave trade as one of the main ways of generating wealth in the country. Blake, like many people in his milieu, wanted the slave trade abolished. It is unlikely that he had met any black people however. While the poem does not appear to be explicitly about the slave trade, this context certainly is important.

The poem is narrated by a little black boy presumably living either in Africa or the Caribbean. He laments the fact that he has "black" skin and says that his soul is "white". He talks about how his mother took him on her lap and pointed to the sun where God lives and says that when the black boy dies, his skin will vanish like a "cloud", and he will become a "lamb" who will rejoice around the golden tent of God. In other words, he will lose his racial characteristics. The little black boy says that having heard this from his mother, he knows that he and little white boys will become as one when they die, and he will stroke the white boy's "silver hair" and "be like him and he will then love me". The poem is a very spiritual poem in that it suggests that our skins, our outward appearances, are like "clouds" which disguise our souls. There is a sense that the black boy is ashamed of his skin; blackness in the poem appears to have connotations of darkness and possibly ignorance while whiteness connotes God and purity. This is troubling and puzzling for a modern reader and yet it is possible that the poem is ironic; that Blake is actually satirizing these sorts of attitudes. To add to the confusion, Blake coloured in different versions of the poem, with one plate showing the boy to be black and another showing him to be white.

Once again, this is a brilliantly rhythmic poem, which has great variety in its lines; tap out a beat to the poem and you'll see that Blake switches rhythms from rising rhythms, which deploy iambs and anapests, to falling ones, which use trochees and dactyls. The poem is largely written in anapests, which is a rising rhythm, and gives the poem its strange spiritual quality; it is as if the black boy is ascending to heaven buoyed by the rhythm of the poem.

Further investigations

This poem is heavily influenced by the thoughts and ideas of the evangelical Christians who opposed the slave trade on religious grounds, including William Wilberforce. Watch the film *Amazing Grace*, which tells Wilberforce's story or learn more about him.

It is also influenced by the strange theology of Swedenborg, who Blake admired for a while but then rejected.

You can compare different versions of the poem here: http://www.blakearchive.org/exist/blake/archive/comparison.xq?selection=compare&copies=all&bentleynum=B9&copyid=songsie.b&java=

The Blossom

Pre-reading
Why do you think blossom is such a powerful poetic image?

Merry Merry Sparrow
Under leaves so green
A happy Blossom
Sees you swift as arrow
Seek your cradle narrow
Near my Bosom.

Pretty Pretty Robin
Under leaves so green
A happy Blossom
Hears you sobbing sobbing,
Pretty Pretty Robin
Near my Bosom.

Questions
Why is the sparrow "merry" do you think?
  Why is the blossom "happy"?
  Whose "bosom" is being spoken about do you think?
  Why is the robin "sobbing"?

How does the mood change in the poem? What is the effect of the rhythm of the poem?

Creative response
Write your own poem or description of blossom.

Analysis
While this is a very short poem, it is a fascinating one. Keynes (p. 135) argues that it is really a description of the acting of making love; the sparrow represents the penis, or, as he terms it, is a "phallic symbol", diving into the blossom, which represents a vagina. Well, that's got you thinking!

There are other possible interpretations. First, let's get clear about what it's about: a sparrow flies as "swift as arrow" into the blossom, which is "near my bosom", while a pretty robin, which is near "my bosom", hears "you" sobbing; this is presumably the robin. As with many of the poems, it's difficult to attribute the pronouns to specific people or things. Is it the "bosom" of the blossom that is being referred to? Or is it the bosom of the poet, or God? There are no easy answers, but there is a strong sense that the natural world is full of movement and emotion: the sparrow is very fast, while the robin is sobbing. Why is there all this movement and emotion? The answer is found when we situate this poem in the context of the whole collection; Blake is painting a picture of innocence here. He is trying to show that innocence involves more than happiness, it involves energy, delight and emotion; it often can involve a "blurring" of agency, that is people and things are inter-changeable; the natural and the human worlds are one. The creator, the blossom, the robin, the sparrow are all part of one creation, sliding and eliding into each other -- hence the confusion over the pronouns.

Further investigations
The illustration for this poem is stunning and has provoked much commentary because it appears to sexualize the blossom. Look at it and say what you think:

http://www.blakearchive.org/exist/blake/archive/comparison.xq?selection=compare&copies=all&bentleynum=B11&copyid=songsie.b&java=

Songs of Innocence and Experience: A Study Guide

The Chimney Sweeper

Pre-reading

What do you know about chimney sweepers? Brainstorm your thoughts.

When my mother died I was very young,
And my father sold me while yet my tongue,
Could scarcely cry weep weep weep weep.
So your chimneys I sweep & in soot I sleep.

Theres little Tom Dacre, who cried when his head
That curl'd like a lambs back, was shav'd, so I said,
Hush Tom never mind it, for when your head's bare,
You know that the soot cannot spoil your white hair.

And so he was quiet, & that very night,
As Tom was a sleeping he had such a sight,
That thousands of sweepers Dick, Joe, Ned & Jack,
Were all of them lock'd up in coffins of black,

And by came an Angel who had a bright key,
And he open'd the coffins & set them all free.
Then down a green plain leaping laughing they run
And wash in a river and shine in the Sun.

Then naked & white, all their bags left behind,
They rise upon clouds, and sport in the wind.
And the Angel told Tom, if he'd be a good boy,
He'd have God for his father & never want joy.

And so Tom awoke and we rose in the dark
And got with our bags & our brushes to work.
Tho' the morning was cold, Tom was happy & warm.
So if all do their duty, they need not fear harm.

Questions

Who is the speaker in the poem? Why is he weeping?

Who is Tom Dacre? Why did he cry?

What did Tom dream about? What does this dream mean do you think?

What Tom learn from his dream? Do you think the ending is ironic, given the beginning of the poem and what we know about Blake's attitude towards child slave labour?

Creative response

Write your own poem about a child or person who is suffering and has a dream that helps him in some way deal with the problem.

Analysis

You can watch a video of me briefly explaining this poem here on YouTube:

http://www.youtube.com/watch?v=7-_qaaMMGK8

This poem is the first poem in the *Songs of Innocence* which paints a highly tragic picture of a young boy's life. In many ways, it is surprising that it is in the *Songs of Innocence* and yet reading the poem carefully you can see why it might be there. It tells not one, but three stories, which are all interlinked. First, there is the story of the narrator, a young chimney sweep, whose mother has died and has been sold into slavery by his father which has led to him becoming a chimney sweep. The repetition of "weep weep weep weep" is extremely powerful and also evokes the familiar cry of the chimney sweeps on the street: "Sweep! Sweep!" The possessive pronoun "your" is effective because you realise that the narrator is addressing the wealthy educated reader of the poem who may well be using slave labour to sweep their chimneys; thus we can see how Blake is aware of how the wealthy people collude with this sort of child labour. The poem then shifts focus to another sweep, Tom Dacre, who once looked like an innocent lamb but had his head shaved so that he could sweep the chimneys; the poem is clearly referencing both *The Shepherd* and *The Lamb* here. The innocent child, the lamb, is being abused by the adult world. The narrator calms down the crying Tom Dacre by giving him reassurance that his hair won't be spoilt.

Songs of Innocence and Experience: A Study Guide

The poem shifts perspective again and we enter Tom's dream and see the extraordinary sights he sees: the chimney sweepers being liberated from their coffins and rising "upon the clouds". They "sport in the wind". The Angel leads them to a paradise quite similar to that evoked in *The Ecchoing Green* with its "green plain" and natural setting, except this place is, of course, the afterlife. The Angel is an ambivalent figure who shows Tom heaven but only promises that he will get there if he is a "good boy". This is the lesson that both the narrator and Tom learn: "if all do their duty, they need not fear harm." Is Blake being ironic here? Having shown with *The Ecchoing Green* and *The Shepherd* that heaven is to be found here on earth in a pastoral idyll (a perfect country setting), he now appears to be saying that children will only get to heaven if they behave themselves. Is Blake showing how the promise of heaven is actually a social control mechanism to get children to do as they are told, and to brainwash them to endure horrific conditions? The ending is very ambivalent. Later on, in the *Songs of Experience*, Blake is very critical of the ways in which the established church tries to control people and children. In *London*, he talks about how the "Chimney Sweepers cry/The blackening church appals", in other words, how the misery of the chimney sweeper shames the church and all it stands for.

This poem has great rhythmic subtlety. It's really worth clapping or tapping the rhythm of the poem because you can see in the pulse how there is a heavy, misery-laden beat which sometimes carries on after the line has finished. The rhythm of each line is four main beats but sometimes you have to carry on tapping out the rhythm of the beat after the line has finished. This is particularly the case with the last line:

So if **all** do their **duty**, they **need** not fear **harm**. (**+ one more beat**)

If you clap the rhythm of this line while reading it, you'll see that you MUST clap a last beat after the line has finished, thus suggesting an absence, a "ghost beat", the ghost of the chimney sweep. The rhythm creates a harsh, heavy rising beat, which is composed largely of anapests (di-di-DUM) and iambs (di-DUM). The uneasy quality of that last line is also created by the half-rhyme which is different from the rest of the poem which contains full mono-syllabic rhymes. Some of the rhymes are very effective: "Jack" and "black" really emphasizes the horror of chimney sweepers' deaths by reminding us that Jack is immersed in the blackness of his coffin and death.

Further investigations

You can compare different versions of the poem here: http://www.blakearchive.org/exist/blake/archive/comparison.xq?selection=compare&copies=all&bentleynum=B12&copyid=songsie.b&java=

A thoughtful response to the poem is here: http://www.socialsciencemedley.com/2011/03/analysis-of-chimney-sweeper-by-william.html

Stewart Crehan writes his book *Blake in Context* (p. 67) that the black coffins in the poem are the tall, black chimneys of London houses and mansions, where many child labourers had died, and that the only freedom from cleaning chimneys was death. He argues that Tom is not actually free at all in the poem, but enslaved by the religious ideology of the time which told children they would go to heaven if they behaved. Blake, for Crehan, didn't believe this, and appears to argue in a subtle way that true freedom comes from freeing yourself from the "dominant ideology". What do you think of Crehan's analysis?

The Little Boy Lost (Innocence)

Pre-reading

Brainstorm the times when you have been lost in your life. What happened? What did you feel and think?

> Father, father, where are you going
> O do not walk so fast.
> Speak father, speak to your little boy
> Or else I shall be lost,
>
> The night was dark no father was there
> The child was wet with dew
> The mire was deep, & the child did weep
> And away the vapour flew.

Questions

Why is the boy upset with his father? Where do you think they are going?

What is happening in the night? What does the night symbolize do you think?

Why has Blake structured the poem in two verses?

Creative response

Using your notes from the pre-reading activity, write a poem about being lost, using striking imagery like Blake does.

Analysis

You can watch a video of me briefly explaining this poem here on YouTube:

http://www.youtube.com/watch?v=QJH1_BcBopk

The theme of "lost" children, initiated by *The Chimney Sweeper*, continues with the *Little Boy Lost*. The poem begins with an alarming cry: "Father, father where are you going"; the two trochaic words "**Fath**er, **Fath**er" create a sense of falling, of loss, which is followed by a dactyl and a trochee: "**where** are you **go**ing" only add to this sense falling and confusion. The poem is directly addressed to the father in the first verse and is mainly composed of trochees and dactyls; falling rhythms. The rhythm captures the bemusement and anxiety of the child. However, the next verse is written from a different perspective: an omniscient narrator (all-seeing narrator) "pans back" like a camera and we watch the child "wet with dew ...weep" amidst the flying "vapour" or fog. The image is that of a boy who is lost on a moor. It is half of the story, but a richly suggestive story though. Has the boy been abandoned by God? Is this who the father is? Or does the boy symbolize children more generally who are abandoned by their parents and adult authority?

Further investigations

You can compare different versions of this poem here: http://www.blakearchive.org/exist/blake/archive/comparison.xq?selection=compare&copies=all&bentleynum=B13&copyid=songsie.b&java=

It's worth comparing this poem with *The Chimney Sweeper* poems, and the other poems about lost children, particularly *A Little Boy Lost* in *Experience*.

The Little Boy Found (Innocence)

Pre-reading

What does it feel like to be found after being lost? What feelings does it evoke in both the finder and the found?

> The little boy lost in the lonely fen,
> Led by the wand'ring light,
> Began to cry, but God ever nigh,
> Appeard like his father in white.
>
> He kissed the child & by the hand led
> And to his mother brought,
> Who in sorrow pale, thro' the lonely dale
> Her little boy weeping sought.

Songs of Innocence and Experience: A Study Guide

Questions

How is the boy rescued?

Why is the boy taken to his mother, and not his father?

There are two fathers in this poem: how do they represent the two sides to fatherhood?

Creative response

Write a poem about being found or a child being found, call it "Found".

Analysis

You can watch a video of me briefly explaining this poem here on YouTube:

http://www.youtube.com/watch?v=QJH1_BcBopk

The poem continues; as with the last verse in the previous poem, we have an omniscient narrator who is describing through the use of powerful visual imagery how lost the child is. He is being led by "the wand'ring light"; this suggests that the "willow-the-wisp" lights of the fen or moor are leading him astray. But a different form of light, the white light of the patriarchal God, appears before him and kisses the child and takes him to his mother – not his father. The representation of fathers and mothers in the poem is fascinating; the boy was abandoned by his father, but found by the fatherly God, who then passes him onto his mother, who was looking for him. In *A Dream* we find the motherly Emmet or Ant searching for her children too in a similarly woebegone fashion. The mother here is "in sorrow pale" and is "weeping" as she seeks her child. We have a picture here of a difficult familial set-up; the careless, neglectful, possibly abusive father, the worried, anxious mother, the lost child.

Further investigations

You can compare different versions of this poem here:

http://www.blakearchive.org/exist/blake/archive/comparison.xq?selection=compare&copies=all&bentleynum=B14&copyid=songsie.b&java=

Do some research into the treatment of children during Blake's life-time.

Francis Gilbert

The Laughing Song
Pre-reading
When do you laugh most? Who makes you laugh? What situations do you laugh in? When is laughter treated positively and negatively?

> When the green woods laugh with the voice of joy
> And the dimpling stream runs laughing by,
> When the air does laugh with our merry wit,
> And the green hill laughs with the noise of it.
>
> When the meadows laugh with lively green
> And the grasshopper laughs in the merry scene,
> When Mary and Susan and Emily,
> With their sweet round mouths sing Ha, Ha, He.
>
> When the painted birds laugh in the shade
> Where our table with cherries and nuts is spread
> Come live & be merry and join with me,
> To sing the sweet chorus of Ha, Ha, He.

Questions
Why are the woods, streams, air and hills laughing here? What is Blake suggesting about nature by personifying it like this?
  Why are "Mary and Susan and Emily" laughing?
  What is the rhythm of this poem and its effects?
  What is Blake saying about laughing and innocence here?

Creative response
Write a poem/description of different times when you have laughed a great deal.

Analysis
You can watch a video of me briefly explaining this poem here on YouTube:
  http://www.youtube.com/watch?v=vRKvKoXUgis

Blake switches mood now and produces one of his most rhythmically joyous poems. This poem really works when you read it aloud and clap the rhythm, it is genuinely like a song; you can just imagine a drum beat making the poem come alive. The poem is largely "anapaestic"; that is, it is full of fast-paced metrical feet called anapests which create a fantastically energetic tone; the rhythm is always "rising". Let's look at the first verse; the heavy beats are in bold:

> When the **green** woods **laugh** with the **voice** of **joy** (anapest, iamb, anapest, iamb)
> And the **dimpling stream** runs **laugh**ing **by**, (anapest, iamb, iamb, iamb)
> When the **air** does **laugh** with our **mer**ry **wit**, (anapest, iamb, anapest, iamb)
> And the **green** hill **laughs** with the **noise** of **it**. (anapest, iamb, anapest, iamb)

The tone here is happy and joyful. Blake uses pastoral imagery to conjure a picture of paradise where, as we saw in *The Ecchoing Green*, both the natural and human worlds are as one; he personifies the woods, the stream, the air, the hills as laughing people who are listening and responding to each other. What a contrast to *The Little Boy Lost* where we saw the father ignoring his child. Blake names three girls, Mary, Susan and Emily and tell us they sing, "Ha, Ha, He." The fact that they are not saying words imbued with meaning is important; they are expressing themselves in a form which is beyond language, but are articulating the joy in their souls. Having done this, the poet invites everyone reading the poem to "come live & be merry and join with me" in the paradise he has created; this is a "painted" world which the poet has created through his art, the birds are painted, or illuminated in Blake's illustrations to the poem. Thus we can see that Blake is arguing that paradise is created by the human imagination and art, and can be accessed any time someone looks at a picture, or reads a poem, or sings "Ha, Ha, He."

Further investigations

You can find the song on the William Blake archive here: http://www.blakearchive.org/exist/blake/archive/object.xq?objectid=songsie.b.illbk.07&java=no. What do illustrations tells us about the poem?

Do some research into what makes people laugh and why laughter is a vital component of human life.

A Cradle Song
Pre-reading

What memories do you have of going to sleep as a young child? Do you have memories of being read to by a parent/grandparent and/or guardian?

>Sweet dreams form a shade
>O'er my lovely infants head.
>Sweet dreams of pleasant streams,
>By happy silent moony beams
>
>Sweet sleep with soft down,
>Weave thy brows an infant crown.
>Sweet sleep Angel mild,
>Hover o'er my happy child.
>
>Sweet smiles in the night,
>Hover over my delight.
>Sweet smiles Mothers smiles
>All the livelong night beguiles.
>
>Sweet moans, dovelike sighs,
>Chase not slumber from thy eyes,
>Sweet moans, sweeter smiles,
>All the dovelike moans beguiles.

Songs of Innocence and Experience: A Study Guide

Sleep sleep happy child.
All creation slept and smil'd.
Sleep sleep, happy sleep,
While o'er thee thy mother weep

Sweet babe in thy face,
Holy image I can trace.
Sweet babe once like thee,
Thy maker lay and wept for me

Wept for me for thee for all,
When he was an infant small.
Thou his image ever see.
Heavenly face that smiles on thee.

Smiles on thee on me on all,
Who became an infant small,
Infant smiles are his own smiles,
Heaven & earth to peace beguiles.

Questions

What words does Blake repeat in this poem and what is the effect of the repetition?

How is this poem structured? Explain and why this poem shifts in focus.

Who is speaking in the poem and what is the speaker's attitude towards their child and to the creator?

Creative response

Write your own *Cradle Song*, but update it so that you protect the child from all the dangers in the modern world.

Analysis

You can watch a video of me briefly explaining this poem here on YouTube:

http://www.youtube.com/watch?v=yKf-VpCneVs

This poem is a lullaby, which could easily be sung. A mother is singing her child to sleep. Many Blakean words and images arise in the poem. Perhaps the first adjective that leaps out when you read the poem is "sweet". This is an important epithet (adjective or describing word) in Blake; we are told that the Shepherd has a "sweet" lot. The adjective has connotations of sugariness, of saccharine, of affection and love. The mother is wishing for "sweet" sleep and dreams for her child; sleep is personified as an Angel which "hovers" over the child. However, while the tone is happy and loving, not everything is as it appears to be:

> Sweet smiles Mothers smiles
> All the livelong night beguiles.

The mother in other words "beguiles" or tricks the child into sleep with her smiles. She is comforting her child by telling her child that the world is safe, when we know, having read *The Little Boy Lost* and *The Chimney Sweeper* etc, that it is not. The mother sees the "Holy Image" in the face of the child; she sees Jesus in her child. This again is a repeated idea in Blake; we saw it in *The Lamb* where we learn that the Lamb, or Jesus, became a child. This idea is developed and explored for the rest of the poem; the links between the baby child and Jesus. We learn that Jesus:

> Wept for me for thee for all,
> When he was an infant small.

Thus the poem which has started as a mother's lullaby for a child has become a lullaby for us all; Jesus "wept for thee for all". *A Cradle Song* is addressed to all of us; it is a song which aims to lull all of us to sleep. But within this lullaby is a dark thread: Jesus "wept" for us. He is crying for our sufferings as well as smiling. Even his smiling is double-edged because it is a form of "beguiling", or charming trickery. Is Blake saying here that in order to sleep peacefully we have to believe in the illusion that all is well, that the world is benign? Is Blake suggesting that sleep is a form of trickery?

Further investigations

Blake created a number of different versions of the poem, which you can compare here:

http://www.blakearchive.org/exist/blake/archive/comparison.xq?selection=compare&copies=all&bentleynum=B16&copyid=songsie.b&java= and here:

http://www.blakearchive.org/exist/blake/archive/comparison.xq?selection=compare&copies=all&bentleynum=B17&copyid=songsie.b&java=

What are the similarities and differences between the versions?

A Cradle Song is based on the structure of Dr. Watt's (1674-1748) *A Cradle Hymn*, however it is very different in tone and approach from this religious hymn, which is about the importance of children obeying God's commandments, rather than being inspired by them. This is the beginning of the poem:

> HUSH, my dear; lie still and slumber
> Holy angels guard thy bed;
> Heavenly blessings, without number,
> Gently falling on thy head.

The critic Zachary Leader notes that Blake borrows from the children's literature of his day, often copying the "form" of certain poems, like the Watt's hymn, but usually reversing the message of such poems. Watt's *Divine Songs* – of which *A Cradle Hymn* is one poem – are full of instructions for children to behave, and to expect punishment if they don't (Leader, p. 34). Blake takes the opposite view and creates a dream-like atmosphere in the poem where the smiles of the child, the mother and God become indistinguishable; they all become one. There are no children or adults in Blake's poem, only common caring humanity. Leader perceives that the spell cast over the mother is only broken when she thinks of the "historical Christ" (p. 100). What do you think of Leader's ideas? How do they change your view of the poem?

Francis Gilbert

The Divine Image (Innocence)

Pre-reading

What are the most important virtues or attitudes of mind to have in life do you think? What are the most noble emotions and ways of living? In a perfect world, how would people behave?

> To Mercy Pity Peace and Love,
> All pray in their distress:
> And to these virtues of delight
> Return their thankfulness.
>
> For Mercy Pity Peace and Love,
> Is God our father dear:
> And Mercy Pity Peace and Love,
> Is Man his child and care.
>
> For Mercy has a human heart
> Pity, a human face:
> And Love, the human form divine,
> And Peace, the human dress.
>
> Then every man of every clime,
> That prays in his distress,
> Prays to the human form divine
> Love Mercy Pity Peace.
>
> And all must love the human form,
> In heathen, turk or jew.
> Where Mercy, Love & Pity dwell,
> There God is dwelling too.

Questions

What do people do when they are distressed, according to Blake? Why do Mercy, Pity, Love and Peace have a "human face"? Why is it important for all of us to love one another and to feel that we are the same?

How does Blake use repetition in this poem and what is the effect of it?

Creative response

John Lennon wrote *Imagine*, Michael Jackson wrote *We Are The World*: can you have a go at writing a song that describes what a perfect world might look like?

Analysis

You can watch a video of me explaining this poem here: http://www.youtube.com/watch?v=D_ZrXk_WIJs

This poem is where Blake lays out his "credo" – what he believes. John Lennon wrote *Imagine* which sets out his beliefs about how we should live, and Blake wrote *The Divine Image*. The poem feels fairly uncontroversial now. Blake is saying things that most liberal humanists would say: that all the religions are the same, that we are all tied together by our common humanity and that we need to believe in the virtues of "Mercy Pity Peace and Love". However, the poem is not without its complexities and contradictions. Blake says that we pray to God when we are in "distress" or are unhappy, and are thankful for these "virtues of delight" which give us comfort in times of need. These virtues are, of course, "Mercy Pity Peace and Love". In other words, the loving God is a form of these virtues. He then points out that when you show these virtues they will "Return their thankfulness": in other words, you will be treated with "Mercy Pity Peace and Love" if you show these virtues to other people. You get what you give. The second verse really lays out Blake's central theme:

> For Mercy has a human heart
> Pity, a human face:
> And Love, the human form divine,
> And Peace, the human dress.

The repetition of "human" is important and makes Blake a "heretic". This is someone who breaks the laws of the church: you could be imprisoned for this in Blake's day. Blake is saying that

God does not exist outside of us, but within us when we show Love, which is the "human form divine", the holy form of humanity. His belief that "all must love the human form,/In heathen, turk or jew" was heretical in his own time because it said essentially that Christians and heathens (anyone who is not Christian) are worshipping the same God when they show "Mercy, Love & Pity".

Further investigations

Blake created a number of different versions of the poem, which you can compare here:

http://www.blakearchive.org/exist/blake/archive/comparison.xq?selection=compare&copies=all&bentleynum=B18&copyid=songsie.b&java=

What are the similarities and differences between the versions?

The companion poem *The Human Abstract* and *The Divine Image* – left out of the final version of the *Songs of Experience* – is fascinating to compare with this poem because it appears to contradict many of the things stated in this poem. For example, Blake is very critical of the concept of "Pity" in that poem, while he celebrates it here. Why do you think this is?

Holy Thursday (Innocence)

Pre-reading

Can you think of any days when children have to perform certain ritualistic activities either in school or outside of it? For example, Founder's Day, or Harvest Festival, or singing hymns/carols. What sort of feelings do these days engender or create? What is your favourite memory of Christmas or Easter time?

> Twas on a Holy Thursday their innocent faces clean
> The children walking two & two in red & blue & green
> Grey headed beadles walkd before with wands as white as snow
> Till into the high dome of Pauls they like Thames waters flow
>
> O what a multitude they seemd these flowers of London town
> Seated in companies they sit with radiance all their own
> The hum of multitudes was there but multitudes of lambs
> Thousands of little boys & girls raising their innocent hands
>
> Now like a mighty wind they raise to heaven the voice of song
> Or like harmonious thunderings the seats of heaven among
> Beneath them sit the aged men wise guardians of the poor
> Then cherish pity; lest you drive an angel from your door

Questions

Why are the children going to St. Pauls?

What do the children look like and how do they behave?

How do they sing? Why does Blake describe them like this, do you think?

How is this poem structured in terms of its use imagery, rhyme and rhythm?

Creative response

Write your own poem or description of a special day such as Christmas or Founder's Day etc. Make it lively: describe the people involved and their attitudes.

Analysis

You can watch me explain this poem on YouTube here: http://www.youtube.com/watch?v=o09Comyv9io

This poem is about an annual event which happened during Blake's lifetime. Johnson and Grant write (p. 32): "Once a year, beginning in 1782, as many as 6,000 homeless children were marched from their charity schools all over London to attend services held in St Pauls' Cathedral. This spectacle in honour of the patrons and founders of the schools took place on a Thursday."

In the poem, it is not mentioned that the children are orphans or that they go to charity schools. Instead Blake focuses upon the children's "innocence" – their backgrounds are not important. He talks about their colourful clothes – "red and blue and green" – and that they are like the "Thames water". As with many other poems, we see here how innocence enmeshes both the natural (the Thames in this case) and human world (the children). The "grey-headed beadles" are possibly sinister presences with their "white wands": they are old men who are "orderlies" or marshals making sure the children are well-behaved. The second verse focuses upon the wonder of the "multitudes" of these children: they are the "flowers of London town". They are like "lambs". They are the embodiments of the Lord, living forms of Jesus. And the sound they make is "like a mighty wind"; once again as with the metaphor of them being like "flowers of London town" and being "like the Thames water", they are compared to natural phenomena. In this case, we gain a sense of their power; they are like a huge tornado in the "harmonious thunderings" they make. The oxymoronic "harmonious thunderings" suggests that the children are both beautiful in the sound that they make, but possibly uncontrolled like thunder. This weather-based metaphor is particularly suggestive of the unpredictability and power of the children. The "aged men" are "beneath" them; they are "wise guardians of the poor". The word "guardian" is double-edged: it connotes both someone who cares and imprisons. There is also the suggestion that these guardians are powerless compared the multitudes of children who contain the power of "a mighty wind", of thunder and of the Thames.

Is the last line ironic or not? I don't know; Blake commands us to "cherish pity", to take it seriously, to believe in it, to nurture it. We have seen in *The Divine Image* that he believes that certain forms of pity are very important, that they are the "human form divine", the embodiment of God. So he could well be saying to the reader that we need to pity the young children. And yet, we have seen that they possibly don't need our pity, but our admiration for their power and energy.

The poem has great rhythmic power as well. It has a "falling rhythm" in the main, deploying trochees and dactyls to create a pulsating, throbbing marching quality which is constantly changing and is quite unpredictable like the children themselves. Analysing the rhythm of the first verse, I have highlighted the heavy beats:

Twas on a **Holy Thurs**day their **inn**ocent **fac**es **clean**
The **chil**dren **walk**ing **two** & **two** in **red** & **blue** & **green**
Grey headed **bead**les **walk**d before with **wands** as **white** as **snow**
Till into the **high** dome of **Pauls** they like **Thames** waters **flow**

The poem has a hallucinatory, fragmented quality about it. The first verse is actually not a proper sentence; there is no "finite" verb. To write the sentence in Standard English, you'd have to say something like "Twas on a Holy Thursday...that children walked two & two". Instead Blake deploys a gerund "walking" to give us a sense of this event being continually in the present, despite the fact that it happens only once a year. This is because possibly innocence is a continual state of becoming, a continual process of acting, doing and creating.

Further investigations

The companion poem in *Experience* is very critical of the church which states boldly that the authorities are reducing "babes to misery" – the very children we see in this poem possibly.

Blake created a number of different versions of the poem,

which you can compare here:
http://www.blakearchive.org/exist/blake/archive/comparison.xq?selection=compare&copies=all&bentleynum=B19&copyid=songsie.b&java=

What are the similarities and differences between the versions?

Night

Pre-reading
What is your attitude towards night? Can you think any special nights in your life? Why did you like them?

    The sun descending in the west,
    The evening star does shine,
    The birds are silent in their nest,
    And I must seek for mine,
    The moon like a flower,
    In heavens high bower;
    With silent delight,
    Sits and smiles on the night.

    Farewell green fields and happy groves,
    Where flocks have took delight;
    Where lambs have nibbled, silent moves
    The feet of angels bright;
    Unseen they pour blessing,
    And joy without ceasing,
    On each bud and blossom,
    And each sleeping bosom.

    They look in every thoughtless nest,
    Where birds are coverd warm;
    They visit caves of every beast,
    To keep them all from harm:
    If they see any weeping,
    That should have been sleeping

They pour sleep on their head
And sit down by their bed.

When wolves and tygers howl for prey
They pitying stand and weep;
Seeking to drive their thirst away,
And keep them from the sheep,
But if they rush dreadful;
The angels most heedful,
Recieve each mild spirit,
New worlds to inherit.

And there the lions ruddy eyes,
Shall flow with tears of gold:
And pitying the tender cries,
And walking round the fold:
Saying: wrath by his meekness
And by his health, sickness,
Is driven away,
From our immortal day.

And now beside thee bleating lamb,
I can lie down and sleep;
Or think on him who bore thy name,
Grase after thee and weep.
For wash'd in lifes river,
My bright mane for ever,
Shall shine like the gold,
As I guard o'er the fold.

Questions

What happens at night according to this poem?
Who moves silently in the night? Who do they protect?
Who are these people not able to protect?
What happens to the sheep if they are killed?
What is it like in heaven? Who rules there?

Why is there no anger in heaven?
Where does the poet lie down to sleep and why?

Creative response

Write your own descriptive poem about night. Describe angels sailing through the streets and looking after people.

Analysis

You can watch a video of me explaining this poem here: http://www.youtube.com/watch?v=U52We1fZ7Zo

This is one of the most mystical poems in the collection. It begins in a relatively conventional fashion describing in the first verse an idyllic night-time scene, the moon is both compared to a flower in a "bower" – a pleasant shady place – and is personified as smiling on the night. But in the second verse we learn that angels are watching over the world:

> Unseen they pour blessing,
> And joy without ceasing,
> On each bud and blossom,
> And each sleeping bosom.

This ties intimately with Blake's own biography because we know that he saw visions of angels during his life, and spoke once of having the angel of his dead brother, Robert, constantly at his side. So the poem becomes visionary having begun in a descriptive fashion. The angels are modeled on the virtues espoused in *The Divine Image* and *A Cradle Song*:

> If they see any weeping,
> That should have been sleeping
> They pour sleep on their head
> And sit down by their bed.

The gift of sleep is important to Blake; it gives people access to an alternate reality, the dream world, which, for Blake, is just as significant as the waking world. We saw this in *The Chimney Sweeper*, where Tom Dacre's dream of angels taking the dead chimney sweepers to heaven gives him hope amidst his miserable existence. In the four verse, the angels try their best to keep evil at bay, as represented by the wolves and tygers, but they can't always do this:

> But if they rush dreadful;
> The angels most heedful,
> Recieve each mild spirit,
> New worlds to inherit.

Here we see that if the beasts of prey "rush dreadful" – in other words attack their prey and kill it – the angel take care to "receive each mild spirit,/New worlds to inherit". In other words, they will enable them to "inherit" a new world, which means basically helping them get to heaven. Once in heaven, the lion, or God, will drive away "wrath" or anger and they will live in the "immortal day" or eternity. The poem ends with the words of the lion:

> And now beside thee bleating lamb,
> I can lie down and sleep;
> Or think on him who bore thy name,
> Grase after thee and weep.
> For wash'd in lifes river,
> My bright mane for ever,
> Shall shine like the gold,
> As I guard o'er the fold.

So the lion will lie down with lamb – something that the Biblical prophet Isaiah said would happen with the coming of the Messiah – and will meditate upon the Godliness of humanity, with his mane having been washed by "lifes river". Possibly this means that having come into contact with humanity, God, the lion, will forever "guard o'er the fold", or always protect humanity.

The poem has a lilting, dream-like rhythm, which is slow and rapturous which helps conjures the mystical quality of the imagery.

Further investigations

Blake created a number of different versions of the poem, which you can compare here:

http://www.blakearchive.org/exist/blake/archive/comparison.xq?selection=compare&copies=all&bentleynum=B20&copyid=songsie.b&java= and here:

http://www.blakearchive.org/exist/blake/archive/comparison.xq?selection=compare&copies=all&bentleynum=B21&copyid=songsie.b&java=

What are the similarities and differences between the versions? It is also worth looking at Blake's depiction of night in poems such as *Introduction to Experience, Earth's Answer, The Sick Rose* and *London*. What is night symbolic and suggestive of in these poems?

Spring

Pre-reading

What is your attitude towards spring? What do you notice happens at spring time? How does your mood and attitude change? Why do you think it used to be seen as a very important time of year but isn't so important to us in the modern world now?

> Sound the Flute!
> Now it's mute.
> Birds delight
> Day and Night.
> Nightingale
> In the dale
> Lark in Sky
> Merrily
> Merrily Merrily to welcome in the Year
>
> Little Boy
> Full of joy.

Songs of Innocence and Experience: A Study Guide

Little Girl
Sweet and small.
Cock does crow
So do you.
Merry voice
Infant noise
Merrily Merrily to welcome in the Year

Little Lamb
Here I am,
Come and lick
My white neck.
Let me pull
Your soft Wool.
Let me kiss
Your soft face.
Merrily Merrily we welcome in the Year

Questions

What happens during spring?
　Why does everyone welcome in the year "merrily"?
　Who does the Lamb lick and why? What does the Lamb symbolize here?

Creative response

Write your own poem about spring in the modern world, describing how people are affected by it.

Analysis

Familiar Blakean themes and images are interwoven with this short, joyous lyric. It is written largely in "trochees", a "falling" rhythm, which creates the halting, choppy rhythm of the poem which helps contribute to the poem's celebratory atmosphere. This is an "annunciation", a bit like a trumpet call, of the advent of spring. The Blakean notions of innocence are present here: the importance of music, the pastoral landscape of the dales, the commonality of the natural world and the human world, the symbolism of the lamb which is suggestive of the best aspects of innocence with its "soft Wool" and "soft face". Human and animal voices and music is important in the poem in much the same way it was in *The Ecchoing Green*. Above all, as with *Laughing Song*, *The Ecchoing Green*, *The Lamb*, we have a mood of joyousness which is best conjured by the repetition of "Merrily" at the end of each verse.

Further investigations

Blake created a number of different versions of the poem, which you can compare here:

http://www.blakearchive.org/exist/blake/archive/comparison.xq?selection=compare&copies=all&bentleynum=B22&copyid=songsie.b&java= and here:
http://www.blakearchive.org/exist/blake/archive/comparison.xq?selection=compare&copies=all&bentleynum=B23&copyid=songsie.b&java=

What are the similarities and differences between the versions?

Nurse's Song (Innocence)

Pre-reading

What are adults' attitudes towards children playing? Can you think of times in your life when you have enjoyed playing and have been told to stop? Do you know of adults who are more "flexible" and more willing to let children play? What do you think of these kinds of adults/teachers?

> When the voices of children are heard on the green
> And laughing is heard on the hill,
> My heart is at rest within my breast
> And everything else is still
>
> Then come home my children, the sun is gone down
> And the dews of night arise
> Come come leave off play, and let us away
> Till the morning appears in the skies

Songs of Innocence and Experience: A Study Guide

> No no let us play, for it is yet day
> And we cannot go to sleep
> Besides in the sky, the little birds fly
> And the hills are all coverd with sheep
>
> Well well go & play till the light fades away
> And then go home to bed
> The little ones leaped & shouted & laugh'd
> And all the hills echoed

Questions

Why is the nurse's heart at rest?
Why does she feel that the children need to go home?
Why do the children want to carry on playing?
What is the nurse's response?
What is Blake trying to say about innocence in this poem do you think?

Creative response

Write a description of or poem about children playing and asking an adult if they can carry on playing.

Analysis

This *Nurse's song* is possibly inspired by the nurses who would take the orphans, who lived in the workhouse that was nearby Blake's childhood home in Soho, to Wimbledon Common so that they could play. The poem opens with the voice of a nurse, or nanny, speaking: she is looking after children who are playing near the hill. The nurse is feeling emotionally calm -- "my heart is at rest within my breast" – and notices that "everything else is still", in other words nature is quiet, possibly the birds have stopped singing. This suggests that the day is drawing to a close. The nurse calls to the children to "come away", to leave the "green", which is redolent of *The Ecchoing Green* where children "sport". The children though reply in the third verse and point out that the world of nature is still awake, the birds "fly", the "hills are all coverd with sheep". As with so many poems, we have a sense that the children are at one with nature. The nurse responds by changing her mind and says that they can play "till the light fades away". The children respond with joy, making the hills "echo". This last image is interesting; do the hills echo because of the children crying out, or are they speaking themselves, echoing the thoughts of the children? The half-rhyme of "bed" and "echoed" draws attention to the uncertainty and fragility of these children's lives, who are at the mercy of adult authority. Here we see that adult authority is benign (nice), but in the companion *Nurse's song* in *Experience* we see a different kind of nurse who won't allow children to enjoy themselves.

Further investigations
It is worth comparing this poem in depth with the companion poem in *Experience*. Blake created a number of different versions of the poem, which you can compare here: http://www.blakearchive.org/exist/blake/archive/comparison.xq?selection=compare&copies=all&bentleynum=B24&copyid=songsie.b&java= What are the similarities and differences between the versions?

Infant Joy

Pre-reading

Think about your attitude towards babies. What do you know about them? What do you think of them? Why do they, for some people, embody innocence? When do babies first learn to smile, to laugh, to walk, to talk? Brainstorm all you know about babies.

I have no name
I am but two days old. --
What shall I call thee?
I happy am
Joy is my name, --
Sweet joy befall thee!

Pretty joy!
Sweet joy but two days old.

Songs of Innocence and Experience: A Study Guide

> Sweet joy I call thee:
> Thou dost smile,
> I sing the while
> Sweet joy befall thee.

Questions

Who are the speakers in this poem?

Why is the baby's name "joy"?

Real babies can't smile at two days old – why has Blake suggested that they can here?

Is he talking about a real baby or a concept?

Why is the poet wishing for the baby to have joy in its life?

Creative response

Write a poem about a baby, describing it in detail. What does your baby embody? What does it symbolize?

Analysis

This short, joyful poem is essentially dialogue between a new born baby and a parent. The poem begins by being spoken in the voice of a new-born child, but then switches voice to that of a parent who asks what the baby should be called. The baby responds by saying his name is "Joy", the parent is taken with this idea and says that the baby's life should be filled with joy. The parent speaks the whole of the second verse having been inspired by the baby's request for the name of Joy. The parent delights in the beauty of the baby and its youth, and says that "sweet joy" should "befall thee". The poem is rhythmically very subtle, with two heavy stresses in each line; it is largely trochaic, with the trochees merging with the simple lexis to create the lilting, tender atmosphere of the poem. This said at certain points the poem switches to a rising rhythm of iambs. We see this most clearly in the last two lines:

I **sing** the **while** (two iambs)
Sweet joy be**fall** thee (a dactyl, trochee)

The switch from the iambs to dactyls and trochees is surprising and helps emphasize the message of hope in the last line because the dactyl and trochee really give the message of hope significance.

Francis Gilbert

Further investigations

Blake created a number of different versions of the poem, which you can compare here:

http://www.blakearchive.org/exist/blake/archive/comparison.xq?selection=compare&copies=all&bentleynum=B25&copyid=songsie.b&java=

What are the similarities and differences between the versions?

This poem has a companion poem in the *Songs of Experience* called *Infant Sorrow*. It is well worth comparing the two poems.

A Dream

Pre-reading

What is your attitude towards dreams? Do you take them seriously? Do they affect you in a profound way? Have you had any memorable dreams that have affected your mood and attitude towards things? Brainstorm all you know about dreams.

Once a dream did weave a shade,
O'er my Angel-guarded bed,
That an Emmet lost it's way
Where on grass methought I lay.

Troubled wilderd and forlorn
Dark, benighted travel-worn
Over many a tangled spray,
All heart-broke I heard her say.

O my children! do they cry,
Do they hear their father sigh.
Now they look abroad to see,
Now return and weep for me.

Pitying I drop'd a tear:
But I saw a glow-worm near:
Who replied, What wailing wight

Songs of Innocence and Experience: A Study Guide

Calls the watchman of the night.

I am set to light the ground,
While the beetle goes his round:
Follow now the beetles hum,
Little wanderer hie thee home.

Questions

Why was the poet's bed "angel-guarded" do you think?

An Emmet is an ant. Why do you think the poet is dreaming about an ant?

The ant is described as being "troubled". Why?

What has happened to her children?

Why do you think a glow-worm replies to the ant? What reassurance does the glow-worm give?

Creative response

Write a poem about a powerful dream you have had. Or write an argumentative piece of writing arguing that we should take dreams much more seriously.

Analysis

You can watch me explain this poem here:

http://www.youtube.com/watch?v=q6wTjovyoQ8

A Dream is a mysterious poem which echoes many of the themes and images we've already found in the *Songs of Innocence*. As has happened in *The Chimney Sweeper* we find a dream dominating the poem; the poet is being guarded by angels, much in the same way that the sleepers are guarded in *Night*. This suggests that the dream he or she has is one which conveys an important message. The poet dreams that an "Emmet" or ant has got lost in the grass that the dreamer is dreaming that he is lying down in. The second verse describes the ant's situation with a series of powerful adjectives: she is "troubled wilder and folorn/Dark benighted travel-worn…all heart-broke". This series of adjectives has a jarring and emotional effect suggesting the extreme confusion, sadness and wretchedness of the ant, which is caught up in a tangled bush or "spray". The ant wails out in the third verse that she has lost her children; she wonders whether they are hearing their father sighing because they have left home – "look abroad to see". She asks for them to "return and weep for me"; to take pity on her and come back home. The dreaming poet cries in his dream about the poor ant and then sees a glow-worm, who is a "watchman of the night" or a sort of policeman. The glow-worm asks what "wailing wight" or moaning person is calling him. He says that he is commanded to light the ground and while the beetle is doing his "round" or beat. He tells the ant to follow the humming beetle and make her way home, presumably where she will find her children – or not. We never quite learn what has happened to them. The poem is fantastical because it is rare enough that you read a poem about a person who is dreaming of lying on the grass and listening to an ant, and even rarer to find the ant as being personified as an unhappy mother, and beetles and glow-worms as policemen. Furthermore, the poem seems to have no resolution; the half-rhyme of "hum" and "home" emphasizes the lack of resolution, the uncertainty of what has happened to the ant. Nevertheless, there is a sense that the glow-worm and beetle have restored some kind of calm to the ant. The poem is written in quatrains with a largely trochaic metre, creating a sense of falling and confusion.

Further investigations

Stewart Crehan in *Blake in Context* argues (p. 102) that all the creatures in this poem care about each other and that they are united by their "compassion". He believes that the parish watch, an early form of policeman, is the "compassionate" glow-worm, and that the parish beadle, a sort of council official, is the "beetle", showing the mother the way back to her family. Crehan puts the case that this poem reminds us about the realities of Blake's London where homelessness was very common. The fact that this is "a dream" is important because it suggests that such caring attitudes don't happen in real life. What do you think of his analysis? Do you think the mother ant is really rescued at the end of the poem? Do you think this poem is really about homelessness in London? Could you interpret the poem in another way?

Songs of Innocence and Experience: A Study Guide

You can find different pictorial versions of the poem here:
http://www.blakearchive.org/exist/blake/archive/comparison.xq?selection=compare&copies=all&bentleynum=B26&copyid=songsie.b&java=

On Another's Sorrow

Pre-reading

What do you feel when you see people you love suffering? What do you feel when you see your enemies suffering? When do you yourself feel sadness and sorrow? Do you feel other people's pain too much? Do you take on their suffering too much? If so, why? If not, why not? Brainstorm or write notes on your thoughts on other people's suffering. Think about when you have seen other people suffer and what your reaction has been.

Can I see anothers woe,
And not be in sorrow too.
Can I see anothers grief,
And not seek for kind relief.

Can I see a falling tear,
And not feel my sorrows share,
Can a father see his child,
Weep, nor be with sorrow fill'd.

Can a mother sit and hear
An infant groan an infant fear --
No no never can it be.
Never never can it be.

And can he who smiles on all
Hear the wren with sorrows small,
Hear the small birds grief & care,

Francis Gilbert

Hear the woes that infants bear --

And not sit beside the nest
Pouring pity in their breast.
And not sit the cradle near
Weeping tear on infants tear.

And not sit both night & day,
Wiping all our tears away.
O! no never can it be.
Never never can it be.

He doth give his joy to all.
He becomes an infant small.
He becomes a man of woe
He doth feel the sorrow too.

Think not, thou canst sigh a sigh,
And thy maker is not by.
Think not, thou canst weep a tear,
And thy maker is not near.

O! he gives to us his joy,
That our grief he may destroy
Till our grief is fled & gone
He doth sit by us and moan

Questions

What does Blake say people feel when they see other people suffering?

What do parents feel when they see their children suffering?

Blake talks about the "maker" in the poem. Who is the "maker"? Why does Blake call him this?

When is God near to people? Why does Blake suggest that God suffers too? What sort of picture is Blake building up of God here?

Blake uses a great deal of repetition in this poem. When and why does he do this, do you think?

Creative response

Write a poem or description of someone else who is suffering in some way, and write about the responses of people around that person. Describe a specific situation and specific characters if you can.

Analysis

You can watch a video of me explaining this poem here: http://www.youtube.com/watch?v=9R0YykBAFXY

This poem which ends the *Songs of Innocence* is about the nature of empathy; Blake argues that humans can't watch someone else suffer and not seek to find "kind relief" for the sufferer. He is positing the case that we are naturally kind-hearted; that we naturally seek to alleviate people's suffering. He feels this is particularly the case with parents watching their children suffer.

> Can a father see his child,
> Weep, nor be with sorrow fill'd.
>
> Can a mother sit and hear
> An infant groan an infant fear –

This is in marked contrast to the attitude towards parents in the *Songs of Experience* where we see in poems like *The Chimney Sweeper, The Little Vagabond, The Nurse's song* and *The Little Girl Lost* parents or guardians behaving in a cruel way towards their children. But Blake is adamant that this can't happen if a parent is truly caring:

> No no never can it be.
> Never never can it be.

The powerful trochaic rhythm of the line emphasizes Blake's absolute certainty that parents have to feel a deep empathy for their children. The second half of the poem shifts its focus to Jesus who feels the suffering of all living things. As we saw in *A Cradle Song*, Jesus is not only full of concern for all living creatures but actually becomes them:

> He becomes an infant small.
> He becomes a man of woe
> He doth feel the sorrow too

This is very striking. Blake's Jesus is a "Protean" creature, who is constantly changing and shape-shifting, and it is precisely this act of "becoming us", of becoming our sorrow that is the nature of his sacrifice for us. Thus we see Blake re-interpreting, in a way, the crucifixion; Jesus's crucifixion was a metaphorical act which means he becomes our misery, thus alleviating us of it:

> Till our grief is fled & gone
> He doth sit by us and moan

Once again, Blake ends the poem on a "half-rhyme" which suggests an uneasy resolution to the poem. The suffering of Christ makes us uneasy because he seems so unhappy at the end of the poem; he is moaning with our grief.

Further investigations

Look at *The Human Abstract* and *The Divine Image* which are very similar poems to this one. You can see different versions of this poem here on the Blake archive:

http://www.blakearchive.org/exist/blake/archive/comparison.xq?selection=compare&copies=all&bentleynum=B27&copyid=songsie.b&java=

Songs of Innocence and Experience: A Study Guide

Francis Gilbert

Songs of Experience – Title page

Look at the title page of this book and think about what the picture suggests about Blake's themes and imagery. What does the title page suggest about the poems that are about to follow?

You can find different versions of the pictures here:

http://www.blakearchive.org/exist/blake/archive/comparison.xq?selection=compare&copies=all&bentleynum=B28&copyid=songsie.b&java=

and here:

http://www.blakearchive.org/exist/blake/archive/comparison.xq?selection=compare&copies=all&bentleynum=B29&copyid=songsie.b&java=

Introduction to Experience

Pre-reading

Think about people you know who seem very wise. What makes them wise? What makes them so "all-knowing"? What qualities do they have that makes them able to predict the future, to analyse the past and present in a clear way? How do they deal with problems? What do they think of the difficult situations in the world today? What are their solutions? What do you think the problems are in the world today? What do you think the solutions are? How is innocence different from experience in your view?

Hear the voice of the Bard!
Who Present, Past, & Future sees
Whose ears have heard,
The Holy Word,
That walk'd among the ancient trees.

Calling the lapsed Soul
And weeping in the evening dew:
That might controll

> The starry pole:
> And fallen fallen light renew!
>
> O Earth O Earth return!
> Arise from out the dewy grass;
> Night is worn,
> And the morn
> Rises from the slumberous mass.
>
> Turn away no more:
> Why wilt thou turn away
> The starry floor
> The watry shore
> Is giv'n thee till the break of day.

Questions

Who is the Bard and what is special about him?

What do you think the "Holy Word" is and means?

Who walked among the ancient trees? Clue: this is probably a reference to the Garden of Eden.

What is a "lapsd Soul" and why can the Bard save him/her?

What is the "fallen light" and how might it be "renewed"?

Why does the Bard call for the Earth to return? Who is the Earth?

Creative response

Write your own poem in which you call for someone to rescue a bad situation. In your poem, describe the situation and explain why things need to change.

Earth's Answer

Pre-reading

When have you felt very miserable? Why have you felt miserable? When have you felt that someone or a situation is "imprisoning" you – either literally or metaphorically? Think about times when you might have been "grounded" or have had a detention, or have

Francis Gilbert

felt trapped in a situation that you can't get out of. What were your feelings? What images might you use to describe your situation?

Earth rais'd up her head,
From the darkness dread & drear,
Her light fled:
Stony dread!
And her locks cover'd with grey despair.

Prison'd on watry shore,
Starry jealousy does keep my den
Cold and hoar
Weeping o'er
I hear the father of the ancient men

Selfish father of men
Cruel jealous selfish fear
Can delight
Chain'd in night
The virgins of youth and morning bear.

Does spring hide its joy
When buds and blossoms grow?
Does the sower?
Sow by night?
Or the plowman in darkness plow?

Break this heavy chain,
That does freeze my bones around
Selfish! vain!
Eternal bane!
That free Love with bondage bound.

Questions
Why is the Earth imprisoned do you think? What does the Earth

symbolize?

Who is the "father of men" do you think?

Why is he imprisoning the Earth? Why is he imprisoning "virgins of youth" and making the spring "hide its joy"?

Why and how does the Earth ask to be freed in the last verse?

Creative response

Write a poem about a person who is trapped in a situation and cries out to be freed. Or write a description of a similar situation. Or write an article about how and why imprisonment occurs.

Analysis

You can watch me explain these poems on YouTube here: http://www.youtube.com/watch?v=xnHSUjymG6U

Blake's *Introduction* to *Experience* has to be talked about together with *Earth's Answer* for a number of reasons. First, it is clear that Blake intended the poems to be put together because the Earth, personified as an unhappy daughter, responds to the subject matter in the *Introduction*. Second, because it becomes clear that what is said in the *Introduction* could be read in an "ironic" light if you take what the Earth says seriously; that is, what you initially think is Blake the poet stating as truth in the *Introduction* may well not be.

Although the *Introduction* is a short poem, it is a complex one. The poet shouts out in the first line that the reader must hear the "voice of the Bard!" The exclamation mark and the capitalization of Bard indicate a forceful, trumpeted opening. The following lines show that the Bard, or holy poet, is a "prophet"; someone who sees the "Present, Past & Future". He has heard the "Holy Word" or the voice of Jesus/God that walked amongst the "ancient trees" of Eden, or Paradise. The next verse is confusing because it's not clear whether it is the Holy Word (God) or the Bard who is calling the "lapsed Soul". The "lapsed Soul" is a "fallen" or "corrupted" spirit, presumably the soul of mankind; this is a common Biblical phrase to describe people who have fallen into sin. We learn that either the Holy Word or the Bard or the lapsed Soul or all of them are "weeping in the evening dew". Again the lack of attribution is very confusing; we are not sure who is being referred to. The poet says that these three are aiming to control the "Starry Pole" and "renew" the "fallen light"; this is obscure imagery again. It possibly suggests that there is an aim to recover the universe from being "fallen".

The third verse contains a cry for the Earth to return and "arise from out the dewy grass". Notice the repetition of the image of the dew; the next three lines suggest that night has passed and the dawn is coming but the Earth is still sleeping as a "slumberous mass". The poet urges the earth not to turn away, and then asks the question about why she is turning away from his commands; he says that the "starry floor" -- the universe -- and the "watery floor" -- the ocean -- is hers until the break of day. In other words, in this time between night and the day emerges, there is a chance for her to rescue herself and mankind from being "lapsed" or "fallen".

The Earth responds in this moment between the night and the dawn; her light has "fled" or departed. She is full of "dread" and her hair "locks" are covered with "grey despair". She imprisoned by the "watry shore" or ocean. God the father, represented by the night-time, or "starry Jealousy", is keeping her prisoner; he is "cruel", "jealous" and he has "chained in night/The virgins of youth". In other words, he is imprisoning young people and the Earth. The next verse questions the wisdom of imprisoning youth and stopping their natural urges; the Earth asks the rhetorical question as to whether the spring "hides its joy" by stopping her "buds and blossoms" growing. Do farmers sow seeds at night and plough in darkness? The answer is obviously no. In other words, the Earth feels that the natural urges of young people are being smothered in darkness and shame. The last verse re-inforces her disgust at what is happening. She has a different command from the Bard and the Holy Word. She wants to break the chains that stop "free Love" from expressing itself. The last verse is a plea for love to be "free"; for people to have sexual relations and/or relationships generally with whom they want. It could also be suggesting that the "virgin" youths of the world, represented by the spring, are stronger than the "father of ancient men"; their imaginative power, like blossoms and buds will inevitably flower, even though the father forbids this. This imagery suggests that the imagination is like nature: it is powerful, beautiful and overwhelming.

Taken together we can see that the *Earth's Answer* clearly contradicts what was said in the *Introduction* because she is so critical of the Bard/Holy Word. Her plea is much easier to understand and less vague.

Further investigations

You can find the different versions of the *Introduction* here:

http://www.blakearchive.org/exist/blake/archive/comparison.xq?selection=compare&copies=all&bentleynum=B30&copyid=songsie.b&java=

while you can find different versions of *Earth's answer* here:

http://www.blakearchive.org/exist/blake/archive/comparison.xq?selection=compare&copies=all&bentleynum=B31&copyid=songsie.b&java=

Both of these poems are heavily influenced by Biblical imagery; it is worth reminding yourself of these (see the section on the Bible).

Francis Gilbert

The Clod & the Pebble
Pre-reading
Who are the most unselfish people you have met in your life? Have you ever noticed that often the most unselfish people are those who have very little and can, at times, be treated quite badly by others? Who are the most selfish people you have met in your life? Have you noticed that often selfish people already have a great deal of money/status/power?

Love seeketh not Itself to please,
Nor for itself hath any care;
But for another gives its ease,
And builds a Heaven in Hells despair.

So sang a little Clod of Clay
Trodden with the cattles feet;
But a Pebble of the brook,
Warbled out these metres meet.

Love seeketh only Self to please,
To bind another to Its delight:
Joys in another's loss of ease,
And builds a Hell in Heaven's despite.

Questions
Why does true love not aim to please itself according to the "Clod of Clay"?
    What is the situation of the Clod of Clay? What do you think the Clod of Clay symbolises?
    Who or what is the Pebble of the Brook? What is his message?
    How do the ideas of the Clod of Clay and the Pebble conflict? Why do they conflict do you think?
Creative response

Write your own fable or symbolic poem about two things that embody selflessness and selfishness. Or write a description of a very selfish person, describing what they say, do and feel. Describe their encounter with a very selfless person. Or write a reflective piece of writing on the times when you have encountered selfishness and selflessness in your life, give the essay the title: "Is it necessary to be selfish to survive?"

Analysis

The poem opens with a Clod of Clay speaking about how someone who really genuinely loves another person does not seek to please him or herself, and shows any care for himself, but instead devotes himself to giving "ease" or comfort to another person. Above all, the person who loves manages to create the feeling of heaven even in a hellish environment; he "builds a Heaven in Hell's despair."

The second verse tells us that it is a "little Clod of Clay" who is singing this song; the Clod is being trodden by the feet of cows who are nearby. In other words, the Clod is oppressed by his surroundings but still finds it in his heart to love others more than himself. Meanwhile, "a Pebble of the brook", or pebble in the stream warbles out a different song. The pebble's "metres meet" or rhythmic verse carries the message that someone who loves actually only is pleasing himself, and aiming to get someone else to help him find delight, such a person enjoys the fact that other people are unhappy, their "loss of ease" and creates a hellish atmosphere where a heavenly one once was.

The Clod's view echoes what St. Paul says of charity in Book 1 of Corinthians, Chapter 13, while the Pebble hints at what Satan says in *Paradise Lost* Book 1, lines 254-55: "The mind is its own place, and in itself/Can make a Heaven of Hell, a Hell of Heaven."

The poem is very carefully structured with the clod's verse being inverted by the pebble in the third verse; much of the lexis is the same but the message of the pebble is the opposite to that of the clod.

Further investigations

You can compare different versions of the poems here:
http://www.blakearchive.org/exist/blake/archive/comparison.xq?

selection=compare&copies=all&bentleynum=B32&copyid=songsie.b&java=

The Clod and the Pebble operates a bit like a fable by Aesop, the Greek writer who wrote a number of stories which carried important messages about how people should treat each other. His stories include *The Tortoise and the Hare* and *The Sun and the Wind*, a fable which is relevant to *The Clod and the Pebble*.

Holy Thursday (Experience)

Pre-reading

Think about all the things you find unfair about the world today. Use these topics as prompts for your thoughts: poverty, exploitation, racism, sexism, child slave labour, starvation, housing, huge differences in wealth, environmental disaster/exploitation, pollution. What are the issues that make you the angriest?

> Is this a holy thing to see,
> In a rich and fruitful land,
> Babes reducd to misery,
> Fed with cold and usurous hand?
>
> Is that trembling cry a song?
> Can it be a song of joy?
> And so many children poor?
> It is a land of poverty!
>
> And their sun does never shine.
> And their fields are bleak and bare.
> And their ways are fill'd with thorns
> It is eternal winter there.
>
> For where-e'er the sun does shine,
> And where-e'er the rain does fall:

Babe can never hunger there,
Nor poverty the mind appall.

Questions

What do the poet suggest is an "unholy" thing to see in England?
What does Blake mean by "eternal winter"?
The last verse is a bit tricky because the poet has turned the "sun" and the "rain" into symbols for fairness and fruitfulness. Explain what you think the last verse means.

Creative response

Write a protest poem which focuses upon one issue that shows people being treated unfairly. Or write an essay or opinion piece entitled "We should be less accepting of unfairness".

Analysis

You can watch a YouTube video of me explaining this poem here: http://www.youtube.com/watch?v=fl_DtGHhbF8

This angry poem is the companion to *Holy Thursday* in the *Songs of Innocence*. Blake opens the poem with an emotional rhetorical question which occupies the first verse, asking whether it is holy to see babies "reduced to misery" in such a land of plenty and being fed, or brought up, by a "cold and usurous hand". He uses the synecdoche (see section on *Analysing language* for more on this) of a "hand" to represent the church, which he describes as both emotionally distant, "cold", and "usurous", which means it is greedy and inclined to selfishly take things from people. The questions continue in the next verse when he asks whether the "trembling cry" is a song. We are reminded of the joyful *Songs of Innocence* such as *Spring* and *Laughing Song*, and we think of the contrast here where the only song being sung is one of fear and poverty. The poet is outraged that so many children are so poor, baldly stating in the last line of the verse that this land is a land of poverty in all senses of the word. The third verse is highly metaphorical: the children never see the sunshine of happiness, of the imagination, they never laugh in the "bleak and bare" fields; they struggle through a thorny landscape, through a life of misery, and live in a winter-time that never ends. The rhyming words "bare" and "there" emphasize the fact that there is only an "eternal winter" in this place.

The final verse says that in a genuinely happy place where the sun and rain exist, there can be no hunger there; the crops will grow and no one will be poor. Of course, the sun and rain are symbols for the happy, "fruitful" life which we saw in the *Songs of Innocence*. The poem is written in four line verses, or quatrains, which employ rhymes in lines two and four, thus giving the poem the quality of a song. The rhyme serve to emphasize Blake's anger; particularly the last ones, with "fall" rhyming with "appall" to create the emphatic, emotional ending which drives home the poet's message that a terrible thing is happening. Quite why the poem is called *Holy Thursday* only makes sense when you read the companion poem in the *Songs of Innocence* which is about how little orphan children went once a year, on a Holy Thursday, to sing in St. Paul's Cathedral to celebrate the founding of their charity schools. That poem was possibly ironic because it presented the children as singing their hearts out, while being supervised by elderly, decrepit men of the established church. Here we see Blake laying the blame for the children's poverty firmly at the church's door; it is the church's "usurous hand" which has led to so many children being poor; the church needs to institute Holy Thursday precisely because there are so many poor children. "Pity would be no more/If we did not make someone poor". They have a culture of charity to alleviate their guilt at having caused the poverty in the first place.

Further investigations

Compare this poem with *Holy Thursday* in *Innocence*.

Find out more about the problems of social inequalities that happened in Blake's day.

http://www.blakearchive.org/exist/blake/archive/comparison.xq?selection=compare&copies=all&bentleynum=B33&copyid=songsie.b&java=

The Little Girl Lost and Found (Experience)

Pre-reading

What do you think the world will look like in 200 years time? Brainstorm your predictions.

In futurity
I prophetic see,
That the earth from sleep,
(Grave the sentence deep)

Shall arise and seek
For her maker meek:
And the desart wild
Become a garden mild.

In the southern clime,
Where the summers prime,
Never fades away;
Lovely Lyca lay.

Seven summers old
Lovely Lyca told,
She had wanderd long
Hearing wild birds song.

Sweet sleep come to me
Underneath this tree;
Do father, mother weep, –
"Where can Lyca sleep".

Lost in desart wild
Is your little child.
How can Lyca sleep,
If her mother weep.

Francis Gilbert

If her heart does ake,
Then let Lyca wake;
If my mother sleep,
Lyca shall not weep.

Frowning frowning night,
O'er this desart bright,
Let thy moon arise,
While I close my eyes.

Sleeping Lyca lay;
While the beasts of prey,
Come from caverns deep,
View'd the maid asleep

The kingly lion stood
And the virgin view'd,
Then he gambold round
O'er the hallowd ground:

Leopards, tygers play,
Round her as she lay;
While the lion old,
Bow'd his mane of gold,

And her bosom lick,
And upon her neck,
From his eyes of flame,
Ruby tears there came;

While the lioness
Loos'd her slender dress,
And naked they convey'd
To caves the sleeping maid.

The Little Girl Found

All the night in woe,
Lyca's parents go:
Over vallies deep,
While the desarts weep.

Tired and woe-begone,
Hoarse with making moan:
Arm in arm seven days,
They trac'd the desart ways.

Seven nights they sleep,
Among shadows deep:
And dream they see their child
Starv'd in desart wild.

Pale thro' pathless ways
The fancied image strays,
Famish'd, weeping, weak
With hollow piteous shriek

Rising from unrest,
The trembling woman prest,
With feet of weary woe;
She could no further go.

In his arms he bore,
Her arm'd with sorrow sore:
Till before their way,
A couching lion lay.

Turning back was vain,
Soon his heavy mane,
Bore them to the ground;

Francis Gilbert

Then he stalk'd around.

Smelling to his prey,
But their fears allay,
When he licks their hands:
And silent by them stands.

They look upon his eyes
Fill'd with deep surprise:
And wondering behold,
A spirit arm'd in gold.

On his head a crown
On his shoulders down,
Flow'd his golden hair.
Gone was all their care.

Follow me he said,
Weep not for the maid:
In my palace deep
Lyca lies asleep.

Then they followed,
Where the vision led:
And saw their sleeping child,
Among tygers wild.

To this day they dwell
In a lonely dell
Nor fear the wolvish howl,
Nor the lions growl.

Questions

Why does Lyca get lost?
 Who finds her?
 Who does the lion symbolize? Look back at *Night* to get some

ideas.

There are many symbols in this poem. What do you think the "desart" and the "cavern" symbolize?

How is Lyca found? Would it be truer to say that her parents are found, rather than they find Lyca? Why might you say this?

Why do all of them stay in this "lonely dell" at the end of the poem? What is this place do you think?

Creative response

After brainstorming some ideas, write your own poem about a little girl who is lost and found. If you like, use ideas you have got from news stories, doing some research if necessary.

Analysis

You can watch a video of me explaining these poems here: http://www.youtube.com/watch?v=pubnHopL_Ww

These two poems are put together on three coloured plates and tell the tale of a seven-year-old girl, Lyca, who lives in the southern hemisphere and becomes lost in the desert. Her parents are very distressed. As Lyca sleeps, she is visited by "beasts of prey", including the "kingly lion" who plays around her, licking her chest and neck, while crying. Getting help from the lioness, they take the naked girl to their caves. The beginning of *The Little Girl Found* focuses upon the parents of Lyca who searching the "vallies deep" and "desarts"; they search for her for seven days and sleep at night. They have a dream that they see her starving in the desert. The mother is "famished, weeping, weak" following Lyca's mirage, her "fancied image"; her husband, the father, has to take her in his arms until they encounter a lion. The lion overwhelms them and looks like he is going to eat them when he begins to lick their hands; they are very surprised and see a golden spirit, with a crown on his head and golden hair flowing down to his shoulders. They lose their worries and follow him, having been told that Lyca is in his palace. When they arrive there they find that Lyca is sleeping with "tygers wild" and have stayed in this "lonely dell" ever since, no longer fearing wild things.

The poem is a parable about how parents learn to become "innocent". Lyca who is seven does not have their anxieties or fears but instead appears to accept the lion's presence without becoming distressed. The parents, in contrast, are overwhelmed by their grief and worry about the loss of their child. The wild animals, and most particularly the lion, are presented as good and spiritual presences in the poem; the lion becomes a golden spirit with long golden hair. He is a Christ-like figure who looks after Lyca by taking her to his cave, and rescues the parents, changing his form so that they will recognize him for who he is; a good spirit.

Further investigations

Different versions of *The Little Girl Lost* are here:
http://www.blakearchive.org/exist/blake/archive/comparison.xq?selection=compare&copies=all&bentleynum=B34&copyid=songsie.b&java=

http://www.blakearchive.org/exist/blake/archive/comparison.xq?selection=compare&copies=all&bentleynum=B35&copyid=songsie.b&java=

Different versions of *The Little Girl Found* can be found here:
http://www.blakearchive.org/exist/blake/archive/comparison.xq?selection=compare&copies=all&bentleynum=B35&copyid=songsie.b&java=

http://www.blakearchive.org/exist/blake/archive/comparison.xq?selection=compare&copies=all&bentleynum=B36&copyid=songsie.b&java=

Songs of Innocence and Experience: A Study Guide

The Chimney Sweeper (Experience)

Pre-reading

Do you think that adults really think about children's happiness? Can you think of times when they put their own selfish interests ahead of children? Do you think our society is structured so that children are a welcome part of it? Are there enough facilities for children etc.? Why do you think children are happy? Can they be happy and yet treated badly?

> A little black thing among the snow:
> Crying weep, weep, in notes of woe!
> Where are thy father & mother? say?
> They are both gone up to the church to pray.
>
> Because I was happy upon the heath,
> And smil'd among the winters snow:
> They clothed me in the clothes of death,
> And taught me to sing the notes of woe.
>
> And because I am happy, & dance & sing,
> They think they have done me no injury:
> And are gone to praise God & his Priest & King
> Who make up a heaven of our misery.

Questions

Who is the "little black thing"? Why does Blake describe him in this way?

Where have the chimney sweeper's parents gone and why have they gone there?

Why has the chimney sweeper been clothed in the "clothes of death"?

Who taught him to sing the "notes of woe"? How does this contrast with the songs in *Innocence*?

Why do "God & his Priest & King" make a "heaven" of the child's misery? Explain these last two lines clearly.

Creative response

Write a description of a child who is neglected by his parents because they are interested in something else other than him, e.g. devoted to a football team, alcohol/drugs, religion etc.

Analysis

You can watch a video of me explaining this poem here: http://www.youtube.com/watch?v=O6-5LqcSOFc

This is the companion poem to *The Chimney Sweeper* in the *Songs of Innocence* and is much more critical of the adult world of experience than the other poem. The poem opens with the poet observing the chimney sweeper as a "little black thing among the snow", immediately painting a poignant picture of a child who has lost his humanity, dignity and parents. He is no more than a "thing" and is "little", indicating that he is malnourished. Furthermore, he is "black", both literally covered in soot, but also he has been made "black" by the church and the world of authority that has engendered this exploitative world. The poet asks the sweep where his father and mother are; they have gone to the established church to pray for their own souls, not his. The next two verses of the poem are spoken in the chimney sweeper's voice. The sweep has been exploited because he was "happy upon the heath" amongst nature and was smiling, despite the fact that it was winter. He is like the Clod of Clay who is trodden under foot but still finds a heaven in hell. As a result, the parents dressed the child in the "clothes of death": they sent him to work in the chimneys to possibly quieten down his natural exuberance and to bring in money for themselves. They also taught him the "notes of woe"; they taught him songs which are the opposite to the ones the Piper sang in the *Introduction* to *Innocence*. They took advantage of the fact that he is "happy", believing that they have done him "no injury", that they have not harmed him. As a result, they have left him weeping amongst the snow so that they can celebrate the world of authority: "God & his Priest & King". This is the patriarchal world of dominance which the Earth found so oppressive in the *Earth's Answer*; this is the selfish world of the "Pebble of the Brook" which only believes in helping itself. Like the Pebble this patriarchal authority makes a "heaven out of our misery", both by enjoying the fact that they are making money out of exploiting their child's labour and "saving themselves" by praying to God.

The poem is structured in an interesting fashion, using four line verses to deliver its points. It has a variable, fluid rhythm which conveys the anger of the poet and the despair of the chimney sweeper; each line of the first verse contains four main beats which reveal the poet's distress at seeing the chimney sweeper so poorly treated. Notice how the heavy beats fall on key words such as "both" and "church" and "woe".

> A **lit**tle black **thing among** the **snow**:
> **Cry**ing **weep**, weep, in **notes** of **woe**!
> **Where** are thy **fath**er & **mo**ther? **say**?
> They are **both** gone **up** to the **church** to **pray**.

Further investigations

You must compare this poem with its companion piece in *Innocence*. You can find different versions of the poem here: http://www.blakearchive.org/exist/blake/archive/comparison.xq?selection=compare&copies=all&bentleynum=B37&copyid=songsie.b&java=

Francis Gilbert

Nurse's Song (Experience)

Pre-reading

Think of teachers/adult you have come across or have heard about who are generally against children playing and don't see the point in play. Why do they think like this? Do they have a point? Brainstorm your ideas.

> When the voices of children, are heard on the green
> And whisprings are in the dale:
> The days of my youth rise fresh in my mind,
> My face turns green and pale.
>
> Then come home my children, the sun is gone down
> And the dews of night arise
> Your spring & your day, are wasted in play
> And your winter and night in disguise.

Questions

How does the attitude of the Nurse here contrast with the attitude of the Nurse in the *Nurse's song* in *Innocence*? How and why do we get a sense of different personalities?

Why does the nurse's face turn "green and pale"? What do these adjectives suggest?

In the *Songs*, Blake often uses the seasons and times of day in a symbolic fashion, what are "spring" and "day", "winter" and "night" symbolic of here do you think?

Creative response

Write a poem or story about an adult who is jealous of children's happiness and stops them playing.

Analysis

You can watch a video of me explaining this poem here: http://www.youtube.com/watch?v=3Akt9IGj9_M

This is the companion poem to the *Nurse's song* in *Innocence*: the first line is the same. We are listening to the voice of a "Nurse" or perhaps in more modern language, a nanny, a person who looks after children. The contrast with the *Innocence* poem is striking in the next line: the children who are cared for by the other nurse are "laughing" but here the children are "whispering", indicating that they may well feel that they are not allowed to laugh out aloud in the presence of this nurse. The nurse has a memory of the days of her youth; unlike the old folk in *The Ecchoing Green*, who remember the days of their youth with fondness and delight, this nurse turns "green and pale". The adjective "green" could possibly reveal that she is jealous in some kind of way of the enjoyment of the children in the dale; or it could be that they are making her feel sick. Unlike the *Innocence* nurse, who allows the children to continue playing because they plead with her, this nurse is quite clear that they must go home. According to the nurse, their time is "wasted in play". For her, these play-times are actually "winter and night in disguise". The striking rhyme of "rise" and "disguise" emphasizes how the nurse feels that joy is a "disguise" for misery; that it is more than useless, it is actually destructive, counter-productive. Once again, we encountering the voice of experience: the jaded voice that far from valuing the joys of youth actually sees them as things to be actively condemned: this is the voice of authority in *The Chimney Sweeper* (*Experience*), the church in *London* and *The Little Vagabond*.

Further investigations

You can find different versions of the poem here:
http://www.blakearchive.org/exist/blake/archive/comparison.xq?selection=compare&copies=all&bentleynum=B38&copyid=songsie.b&java

Francis Gilbert

The Sick Rose

Pre-reading

What do roses symbolize for you? What do worms symbolize? What do they suggest?

> O Rose thou art sick.
> The invisible worm,
> That flies in the night
> In the howling storm:
>
> Has found out thy bed
> Of crimson joy:
> And his dark secret love
> Does thy life destroy.

Questions

Why is the Rose "sick"?

Who or what is the "invisible worm"?

What do "night" and the "howling storm" connote or symbolise?

What is suggested by the "bed/Of crimson joy"?

Why is the Rose's life being destroyed by the invisible worm?

Why is this poem so short?

How does Blake use rhyme and rhythm in this poem?

Creative response

Write your own "symbolist" poem; choose some objects that are obviously symbols for some idea or concept, but do not reveal in the poem what the symbols correlate with. Use personification and the structure of Blake's poem to help you, e.g. "Oh washing machine/You are weak/The invisible rust/That corrodes the night/Has found your pool/Of watery joy/And does with dark secret jealousy/Your life destroy." You can be more imaginative than this, but do you get the idea?

Analysis

Songs of Innocence and Experience: A Study Guide

You can watch two videos of me explaining this poem here:
http://www.youtube.com/watch?v=r1ZaiM2ybX8
& here: http://www.youtube.com/watch?v=p7vqS58arHU

    This is one of Blake's shortest poems, but also one of his most mysterious. Blake personifies the "Rose" as being "sick"; the poet addresses the "Rose" as "thou", the familiar form of you, as though the poet knows the Rose well. The poet then tells us that "the invisible worm" has "found out thy bed/Of crimson joy". Who is this "invisible worm"? Clearly, it is a very sinister and unseen force. Rather like the "mind-forged manacles" and the "Human Abstract" the worm is a construct of the mind that can't be seen but certainly can be felt. Like the Nurse in the previous poem, the worm destroys "joy", which here is described as "crimson" or bright red. The colour scheme of both the poem and the plate is deeply suggestive; many critics have pointed out the sexual symbolism of the poem. The worm could be a phallic image, a symbolic representation of the penis, which is destroying the sexual joy of the Rose. The worm has a "dark secret love". These adjectives are important; "dark" in Blake is nearly always a darkness of the mind, indicating a negative attitude towards life. The worm's secrecy suggests that he is nefarious and under-hand in his dealings with the Rose. His love has not been revealed to the Rose; it is secret and sinister. Here there is a strong link with *A Poison Tree*, which tells another symbolic story about a person who kills his enemy by pretending to like him and as a result a "poison tree" grows in the garden. This poison tree is a representation of his inner, repressed anger or wrath for his enemy. The enemy eats the fruit of the tree believing the tree to be the tree of his friend, but because the fruit is the manifestation of the narrator's poisonous, secret anger, it is deadly and he dies after eating it. Again we have the idea of secrecy destroying joy. The poem is a perfect example of how symbolism works: clearly the "Rose" and the "invisible worm" are symbols for something else -- an idea, a concept, a feeling -- but we never actually can fully work out what they are. The poem makes sense, but only just; it stands on the very edge of meaning. This tantalizing quality is what makes it such a successful poem; its very inscrutability is what makes it so intriguing.

Further investigations
It is worth comparing this poem with the other poetry which uses flower symbolism. In Innocence, *Blossom* and *Spring* are worth looking at, while *My Pretty Rose Tree, Ah! Sunflower*, and *The Lilly* are all similar in imagery and themes to this poem. You can find different versions of the poem here:

http://www.blakearchive.org/exist/blake/archive/comparison.xq?selection=compare&copies=all&bentleynum=B39&copyid=songsie.b&java=

The Fly
Pre-reading
Think about all the creatures in your life that irritate and annoy you: spiders, flies, midges, mosquitoes etc. Why do you have these attitudes towards them?

Little Fly
Thy summers play,
My thoughtless hand
Has brush'd away.

Am not I
A fly like thee?
Or art not thou
A man like me?

For I dance
And drink & sing:
Till some blind hand
Shall brush my wing.

If thought is life
And strength & breath:

And the want
Of thought is death;

Then am I
A happy fly,
If I live,
Or if I die.

Questions

Why is the poet very similar to the fly?

Why does the poet believe "thought is life"? What do you think of this comment?

Why does it follow if "thought is life" that the poet is a "happy fly"? Explain the connection and comparison.

Creative response

Write your own poem in which you address an insect or animal that really irritates you, imagining that it is a bit like you. In what ways would it be like you?

Analysis

You can watch a video of me explaining the poem here: http://www.youtube.com/watch?v=ngUrG4uxcoA

The poet addresses a fly, asking him and us whether he is like a fly like him, and whether the fly is rather like a man. He goes on to explain what he means in the following verses: he, as a man, enjoys dancing, drinking and singing until a "blind hand" or fate brushes his wing and leaves him dead. He then develops a philosophical argument from this point by saying if everything that is alive is a creation of the human mind -- is a "thought" in the human mind -- and the lack of thought is "death", then he is a bit like the fly because he has thoughts which indicate that he is alive, and when he has no thoughts he will be dead. Blake has taken some ideas from certain philosophers here. The French philosopher, Descartes, famously said "cogito ergo sum" -- I think therefore I am – thereby saying that thought is the essence of life. Other philosophers that Blake read such as Bishop Berkeley developed the idea of "idealism", namely that everything that exists is a human construction or a creation of the mind. In other words, Berkeley and Blake believed that it is the human imagination which has labeled, ordered and structured the world with its language; what we see is simply our creation; our brains have brought the world into being, given it order and structure. So we can see that in a very short poem Blake is exploring some serious philosophical issues.

Further investigations
It is well worth looking at the philosophy of Descartes and Bishop Berkley to learn more about their philosophy: *The Oxford Companion to Philosophy* is a good place to start. You can find different versions of the poem here:

http://www.blakearchive.org/exist/blake/archive/comparison.xq?selection=compare&copies=all&bentleynum=B40&copyid=songsie.b&java=

The Angel
Pre-reading
Have you thought what your life would be like if you were a different sex? Have you ever dreamed of having a different social status, e.g. being a "queen"? How would you behave? What would life be like? Would your life be better or worse do you think?

> I Dreamt a Dream! what can it mean?
> And that I was a maiden Queen:
> Guarded by an Angel mild:
> Witless woe, was neer beguil'd!
>
> And I wept both night and day
> And he wip'd my tears away
> And I wept both day and night
> And hid from him my hearts delight
>
> So he took his wings and fled:
> Then the morn blush'd rosy red:

Songs of Innocence and Experience: A Study Guide

> I dried my tears & arm'd my fears,
> With ten thousand shields and spears.
>
> Soon my Angel came again:
> I was arm'd, he came in vain:
> For the time of youth was fled
> And grey hairs were on my head

Questions

Why was the poet tricked or "beguiled" in the dream?

Why did the poet, dreaming that he was a queen, cry in his dream?

Why did the queen hide his "hearts delight" from the angel?

Why did the angel leave?

What does the poet mean when he talks about arming his fears with "ten thousand shields and spears"?

Why does the angel return?

What has happened at the very end of the poem?

What does this dream mean, do you think?

Creative response

Write your own poem about a dream when you become a different gender and different social status.

Analysis

You can watch a video of me explaining this poem here: http://www.youtube.com/watch?v=DHrkA653m0A

Like *A Dream* in *Innocence*, this poem is almost entirely the description of a dream. Blake, as we have seen, believed in the importance of dreams to convey important truths about life. The narrator of this poem becomes a "maiden Queen", in other words, a virgin who rules over a land. Like the narrator in *A Dream* she is guarded by an Angel who is "mild", but as she informs us, it was to no avail. There was no point in the Angel guarding her, there was never someone who was more "beguiled" – tricked by charm -- than she was. The narrator was very depressed, crying day and night, while at the same time hiding from the Angel her true affections. As a result, the Angel flew away, and this made the

Queen angry because he had abandoned her. So the Queen stopped crying and readied herself to fight anyone who might come close to her. When the Angel reappears, the Queen is "armed"; she sends him packing. The poem ends on a note of regret; the Queen has grown older and has found out that her "youth" has fled in much the same way the Angel fled when she cried so much and never revealed her true feelings. The poem is structured in four verses each with four lines each which deploy rhyming couplets: it has the typical structure of a ballad, but as with most of Blake's poems the traditional form is only a starting point for his explorations.

Further investigations

It is well worth exploring Blake's representation of angels in his poetry; look at *Introduction to Innocence, Night, A Dream* and *A Cradle Song.* You can find different versions of the poem here:

http://www.blakearchive.org/exist/blake/archive/comparison.xq?selection=compare&copies=all&bentleynum=B41&copyid=songsie.b&java=

The Tyger

Pre-reading:

What are the most frightening concepts you can think of? What are the most frightening animals? What are the most frightening things that can happen to you? What in your mind embodies evil?

> Tyger Tyger, burning bright,
> In the forests of the night;
> What immortal hand or eye,
> Could frame thy fearful symmetry?
>
> In what distant deeps or skies,
> Burnt the fire of thine eyes?
> On what wings dare he aspire?
> What the hand, dare sieze the fire?

Songs of Innocence and Experience: A Study Guide

And what shoulder, & what art,
Could twist the sinews of thy heart?
And when thy heart began to beat,
What dread hand? & what dread feet?

What the hammer? what the chain,
In what furnace was thy brain?
What the anvil? what dread grasp,
Dare its deadly terrors clasp?

When the stars threw down their spears,
And water'd heaven with their tears:
Did he smile his work to see?
Did he who made the Lamb make thee?

Tyger Tyger burning bright
In the forests of the night:
What immortal hand or eye,
Dare frame thy fearful symmetry?

Questions

Why does Blake spell "tyger" in the way he does?
Why does the tyger burn bright?
What are forests of the night, do you think?
What does Blake mean by "immortal symmetry"?
Why does Blake ask the question about what made the tyger, do you think?
What are the "wings" that the tyger aspires or aims to have?
Why might the tyger's eyes be burning in the deeps of the ocean or the sky? What creature or concept is Blake talking about here, do you think?
Blake asks the question as to what made the "sinews" of the tyger's heart. Sinews means muscles. Why might Blake be talking about the muscles of the tyger's heart?
Why was the tyger's brain made in a furnace?
What is happening when the stars "threw down their spears"?

Why does Blake ask the question as to whether God smiled when he made the tyger?

Why does Blake ask so many questions in this poem?

The last verse is the same as the last verse except for one word. What word has been changed and why?

Creative response

Write your own poem about a truly frightening animal, spectacle or idea – such as the end of the world. Use Blake's structure of asking questions about this animal/concept/spectacle.

Analysis

You can watch a video of me explaining this poem here: http://www.youtube.com/watch?v=q9LFhP38b10

This is possibly Blake's most famous poem and yet it remains one of his most inscrutable lyrics; its meanings are difficult to decipher. This said, the tone and atmosphere of the poem is unmistakeable and is generated by the powerful, mysterious images and stalking, thumping trochaic rhythm.

First of all, let's go through what the poem is about. The poet addresses the "tyger" in the first verse, using the familiar possessive pronoun "thy" to address the animal with. The poet describes how the tyger is "burning bright", in other words seems to be on fire or illuminated in "the forests of the night". Notice how this is a metaphorical forest, not a literal one: the "tyger" inhabits the thickets and "tangled sprays" of the night. If we put the poem in the context of the *Songs of Experience* we can see that this is a recurring image. In *The Human Abstract*, *The Voice of the Ancient Bard* and *The Garden of Love* there are repeated images of nature as being impenetrable, as being "tangled up", as being "forest-like". The tyger is an animal or concept which traverses these domains, which enjoys the secretive, tree-like environment of the dark night. He is an animal of experience. The poet then asks what "immortal hand or eye" made or "framed" the creature. This question is never satisfactorily answered. We never know what made the tyger in the poem.

The next four verses are a series of questions which delve deeper and deeper into the mystery of the creation of the tyger, while giving us more of an idea of the terrific power and passion of the tyger. In the second verse, the tyger's are eyes characterized as volcanic fires under the sea – living in the "distant deeps" – and as suns or stars in space or "skies". The ambition of the tyger is suggested by the question which asks what "on what wings dare he aspire?" We have a sense that the tyger is aiming to fly high above mankind here. Then the poet asks "what hand" or person might "dare sieze the fire", presumably this is the fire of the tyger or its passionate nature; in other words, what person could possibly challenge the fiery passion of the tyger? Equally, it could be asking the question as to what "hand" seized the fire in order to make the tyger? The exact meaning of the line remains very ambivalent.

The next two verses focus more obviously on the creation of the tyger by asking what "shoulder & what art" could have made the muscles of the tyger's heart? This is possibly suggesting that the poet is as afraid of the creator of the tyger as he is of the tyger himself. The imagery in these two verses is that of the creator being a blacksmith making or hammering out the tyger on a forge. Blake, in other poems, personifies the imagination as a blacksmith called Los (*sol* is Latin for sun, spelt backwards). Here we have a sense that the tyger is the product of a mighty and feverish imagination which sculptured the tyger's brain in a furnace with his implements – the "chain" and the "hammer". The last lines of the fourth verse returns to a repeated idea: "what dread grasp,/Dare its deadly terrors clasp?" As we saw at the end of the second verse, the poet has as many questions for the creator of the tyger as the tyger himself: what person could possibly "clasp" the terrors of the tyger? What person or creator is its equal?

The next verse paints an apocalyptic picture of the stars "throwing down their spears", thus personifying the stars as soldiers who are giving up the fight, surrendering their weapons and crying about their defeat, watering "heaven with their tears". Presumably they are doing this because they know that the tyger will always defeat them; that they will never dominate such a powerful creature. Blake asks the question as to whether the creator smiled at the terror of his creation? How could the God that made the Lamb make the tyger? Notice that the poet addresses the tyger in the most direct way possible at this point, calling him "thee". Until now he has only used the possessive pronoun to address the tyger, using the word "thy", but at this point, he seems to look the tyger in the face and say how could the creator who made such an innocent thing as the Lamb also make something so destructive, passionate and powerful as the tyger?

The last line is exactly the same as the first verse except that the conditional verb "could" has been replaced with "dare". We have a sense that as the poem has progressed the poet has become more and more suspicious of the creator's purposes; how could he have the "courage" or nerve to produce something so destructive?

The poem's rhythm is tremendously powerful, mimicking the prowling pace of the tyger in many ways, but also the thumping of the hammer that created the tyger. The metre is largely trochaic, but if you look carefully at the poem, you can see that the rhythm changes, which creates a jarring, disturbing effect:

> **Tyg**er **Tyg**er, **burn**ing **bright**, (four trochees)
> **In** the **for**ests **of** the **night**; (four trochees)
> **What** im**mort**al **hand** or **eye**, (four trochees)
> Could **frame** thy **fear**ful **sym**metry? (four iambs)

The switch to the iambic rhythm in the last line creates a jarring effect as does the half-rhyme of "eye" and "symmetry", thus making us think much more seriously about the question of the creator's intentions when he made the tyger.

Further investigations

In his *Introduction to the Cambridge Companion to William Blake*, Morris Eaves notes that it's "tough" to explain the poem other than on its own terms (p. 4). Do you agree with this point? Does the poem create its own form of creative questioning which means it is impossible to say what it is really about? Crehan meanwhile examined the pamphlets that were being written during the time of the writing of the poem and found that the French "mob" who killed the French monarchy in their revolution was referred to as a "tygerish multitude" which showed the "wanton cruelty of the Tyger" (p.127). He also unearthed the fact that the pamphlet which criticized the French revolutionaries so strongly used the same spelling for the "tyger" as Blake did. In other words, he argues that the poem is deeply political in that the tyger represents the forces of the working classes who wish to overturn the ruling order in a violent fashion. What looks like a mystical poem is actually a coded call for the people to rise up against the vicious social order which created the conditions we see in *London*. Or is it? What do you think of these comments? As Eaves says the poem is so ambiguous that you can virtually put what interpretation you like upon it. That said, read within the context of the other poems in the *Songs of Experience* the case for it being a political poem is not without merit.

What do you think of these comments?

You can see different pictorial versions of this poem here:
http://www.blakearchive.org/exist/blake/archive/comparison.xq?selection=compare&copies=all&bentleynum=B42&copyid=songsie.b&java=

It is also worth looking at Blake's note book and seeing how he revised the poem:
http://www.bl.uk/onlinegallery/ttp/blake/accessible/folion113andn112.html

My Pretty Rose Tree, Ah! Sun-Flower, The Lilly

Pre-reading

What is your attitude towards free love and sexual promiscuity? How important is sexual fidelity in a relationship? What are your reasons for your thoughts? Do you think it's best to wait for the perfect person to come before having a sexual relationship, or do you think you should be able to "experiment"?

Francis Gilbert

My Pretty Rose Tree

A flower was offer'd to me:
Such a flower as May never bore.
But I said I've a Pretty Rose-tree,
And I passed the sweet flower o'er.

Then I went to my Pretty Rose-tree:
To tend her by day and by night.
But my Rose turnd away with jealousy:
And her thorns were my only delight.

Ah! Sun-flower

Ah Sun-flower! weary of time,
Who countest the steps of the Sun:
Seeking after that sweet golden clime,
Where the travellers journey is done.

Where the Youth pined away with desire,
And the pale Virgin shrouded in snow:
Arise from their graves and aspire
Where my Sun-flower wishes to go.

The Lilly

The modest Rose puts forth a thorn:
The humble Sheep, a threatning horn:
While the Lilly white, shall in Love delight,
Nor a thorn nor a threat stain her beauty bright.

Questions

Why do you think Blake put all of these poems on the same plate? In what ways are they linked?

What does the poet possibly mean when he says that a flower was offered to him in *My Pretty Rose Tree*? Why does he reject the offer of the flower? What are the consequences of his rejection of the offer? Why do you think the Rose Tree was jealous?

Why is the Sun-flower weary of time? How does the Sun-flower spend its time? What destination is the Sun-flower seeking? What happens in this place? Why do a Youth and "pale Virgin" live there?

Why is the Lilly different from the Rose Tree and the Sun-flower? Why can no thorn or threat "stain her beauty bright?"

What might Blake be saying about relationships, especially sexual relationships, in this poem?

Creative response

Write your own poems or stories about a jealous partner (*My Pretty Rose Tree*), a person who dreams in vain of having a perfect relationship (*Ah! Sunflower*), and a person who has lots of partners but always remains innocent (*The Lilly*).

Analysis

You can watch a video of me explaining *My Pretty Rose Tree* here: http://www.youtube.com/watch?v=-vs4wN057Uc

Ah! Sunflower here: http://www.youtube.com/watch?v=a9qO6ExhlI4

The Lilly here: http://www.youtube.com/watch?v=qc2-Yb54c80

These three poems are on the same plate and are worth discussing together because they explore similar themes connected with relationships and sex. In *My Pretty Rose Tree* the poet talks about how he was offered a beautiful May flower but he turned the offer of the flower down, only to find when he returned to his Pretty Rose Tree that she was jealous and, as a result, the poet has only found pleasure in the pain of her thorns. As with *The Sick Rose* this is a highly symbolic poem which could well be about the nature of sexual love; the poem appears to be advocating the case for free love. The poet suffers because he turns down the tempting offer of the May flower only to find that when he returns to his regular partner, the Rose Tree, he is rebuffed by her jealousy. Possibly thoughts of the May flower are filling his head and, having not "enjoyed" the May flower, his fantasies of what might have been are poisoning his relationship with the Rose Tree and making that very painful. In *Ah! Sunflower* we learn about another flower which is yearning to be in another place, which is passing the days away "seeking after the sweet golden clime" where all journeys come to an end, possibly looking for some kind of heaven. The second verse tells us about this world which is characterized by repressed desire; it is a place where young people or "Youth pined away with desire", in other words a place where a young people can't find expression or outlets for their desires. As a result, the Virgin remains "shrouded in snow"; she finds no fulfillment in her life and suffers a form of death, being "shrouded" like a dead body by snow, or emotional coldness. The third line tells us that "Youth" and the "Virgin" arise from their graves in this place and are seeking a better life because they "aspire" to something, but whether they find satisfaction or not we don't know. The poem ends by the poet telling us that this spooky, frustrating world is where the poet's Sunflower wishes to go. Again we have, as with *My Pretty Rose Tree*, a picture of a relationship which has gone wrong because one of the partners is dreaming of being somewhere else. *The Lilly* is the most positive poem because even though the Rose may put "forth a thorn", even though the Sheep may have a "threatning horn", the Lilly remains pure whatever she does; there is a suggestion that because she retains an innocent state of mind, the type of mind Blake talks about in the *Songs of Innocence*, she remains pure, even though she might have relationships which many other people deem inappropriate or corrupting.

Taken together these poems develop Blake's ideas about sexuality and relationships. It appears that relationships are ruined not by sex or desire, but by the repression of desire which leads to people opting to believe in fantasy worlds or fantasy people that destroy relationships in the real world: the poet in *My Pretty Rose Tree* does not have sex with the May flower but his relationship with the Pretty Rose tree is ruined anyway because her of jealousy about his desire for the May flower, while the poet in *Ah! Sunflower* has to suffer a relationship with a person who is dreaming of living in a place where desires are hidden or repressed.

Further investigations

It is worth comparing these poems with *The Sick Rose*, *The Angel*, *Spring* and *Blossom*. Why does Blake use the imagery of flowers to explore sexual and psychological themes do you think? You can compare different versions of the poems here:

http://www.blakearchive.org/exist/blake/archive/comparison.xq?selection=compare&copies=all&bentleynum=B43&copyid=songsie.b&java=

The Garden of Love

Pre-reading

Have you ever re-visited a place and found that it has been ruined or that your attitudes towards it have changed? For example, think of re-visiting your old school, or going back on holiday to a place that you really loved as a child; describe your feelings before and after your visit.

I went to the Garden of Love.
And saw what I never had seen:
A Chapel was built in the midst,
Where I used to play on the green.

And the gates of this Chapel were shut,
And Thou shalt not, writ over the door;
So I turn'd to the Garden of Love,
That so many sweet flowers bore,

And I saw it was filled with graves,
And tomb-stones where flowers should be:
And Priests in black gowns, were walking their rounds,
And binding with briars, my joys & desires.

Questions
Why is the poet so shocked in this poem?

Why is the Chapel shut? Why is "Thou shalt not, writ over the door"? Has this literally happened, or is this scene a representation of change in spirit?

Why are there graves on the Green? What do they symbolize?

Why are "Priests in black gowns...walking their rounds"?

Why and how are the poet's "joys & desires" being bound or stopped by "briars"? What is the poet talking about here?

Creative response
Write your own poem about a place that has been ruined or changed greatly from when you first visited it.

Analysis
You can watch a video of me explaining this poem here: http://www.youtube.com/watch?v=oHubXVjsj9g

This poem possibly sums up a central idea in the *Songs of Experience*: the world of *Innocence* has been destroyed by the adult world of authority. The poet opens the poem by describing his dismay at seeing what "I never had seen": the world of *The Ecchoing Green* has been destroyed because a Chapel has been built "where I used to play on the green". The gates of the Chapel are symbolically shut: in other words, children are barred from playing there. The Biblical injunction "Thou shalt not" is "writ over the door"; the church has established a new world of prohibitions, of rules and restrictions which have destroyed the "sweet flowers" of *The Ecchoing Green*. These flowers are both literal and symbolic; the Chapel has literally destroyed the natural world around it with its graves and tomb-stones, but it has also destroyed all that nature used to mean, it has destroyed the freedom of thought and imagination that the world of nature once symbolized. There are now "Priests in black gowns" who are patrolling the area, "walking their rounds", and they are "binding with briars, my joys and desires". They imprisoning people's wishes with their rules and regulations, with their Biblical commandments.

Here you could argue that Blake is writing his own version of "the Fall". The Garden of Eden which was represented by *The Ecchoing Green* has now become "Fallen" because the world of religious adult authority has crushed people's "joys & desires".

The poem's structure is fascinating. It starts off like a traditional ballad, telling the story of the poet visiting a place he used to know but instead of telling a story the second verse contains a description of a place which is animated by a fast-paced anapestic rhythm:

> And the **gates** of this **Chap**el were **shut**, (three anapests)
> And **Thou** shalt **not**, writ **over** the **door**; (three iambs, one anapest)
> So I **turn'd** to the **Gard**en of **Love**, (two anapests, one iamb)
> That so **man**y sweet **flow**ers **bore**, (one anapest, two iambs)

Notice how the second line of the verse contains four harsh beats compared with the other lines which are three beat lines; this is deliberate because Blake is emphasizing the horror of "Thou shalt not" which is further emphasized by the caesura in the middle of the line, which forces the reader to take a pause before continuing with the poem.

Further investigations

It is worth thinking hard about the nature of Blake's non-conformist Christianity. Although his poetry is full of Christian imagery, you could argue that he is actually not a Christian at all; after all, he rejects much of the Bible, doesn't appear to believe in an external, all-seeing God, and rejects the notion of Christ's crucifixion. You can find different versions of the poem here: http://www.blakearchive.org/exist/blake/archive/comparison.xq?selection=compare&copies=all&bentleynum=B44&copyid=songsie.b&java=

Francis Gilbert

The Little Vagabond

Pre-reading

What do you think some similarities and differences between the pub and the church are? Why do they exist as social institutions? What are your attitudes to them?

Dear Mother, dear Mother, the Church is cold.
But the Ale-house is healthy & pleasant & warm:
Besides I can tell where I am used well.
Such usage in heaven will never do well.

But if at the Church they would give us some Ale,
And a pleasant fire, our souls to regale:
We'd sing and we'd pray all the live-long day:
Nor ever once wish from the Church to stray.

Then the Parson might preach & drink & sing,
And we'd be as happy as birds in the spring:
And modest dame Lurch, who is always at Church,
Would not have bandy children nor fasting nor birch.

And God like a father rejoicing to see,
His children as pleasant and happy as he:
Would have no more quarrel with the Devil or the Barrel
But kiss him & give him both drink and apparel.

Questions

What are the differences between the church and the ale house which the Little Vagabond describes here?

Why is the poem called *The Little Vagabond*?

Why might the children be much happier if the Parson preached in the ale-house?

What is the problem with dame Lurch? Why would she not be a problem if the church services were conducted in the ale-house?

Why would the children have no more quarrel with the Devil

and Barrel if their services were in the ale-house?

Who would they give drink and clothes to, and why?

Creative response

Write a poem about the differences between the church and a pub. Or write a poem about either the church or the pub. Or write a descriptive account of one of these places. Or write an article or speech about why we need to be more sociable and develop more institutions which bring people together.

Analysis

You can watch a video of me explaining this poem here: http://www.youtube.com/watch?v=nwuPkJ4DnzQ

Following on as it does from *The Garden of Love*, we find Blake amplifying his theme of the pernicious (damaging) effects of the church. This poem humanizes the issue even more emotionally than we found in *The Garden of Love*. The poem is spoken in the voice of the Little Vagabond, a small homeless boy. He addresses his mother desperately to begin with telling her that the church is cold, whereas the Ale-house or pub is "healthy and warm". He knows that he is treated "well" in the Ale-house and that it is obvious that in Heaven it will be more like the Ale-house than the church. The Little Vagabond then proposes an alternative vision for the church: if they gave everyone some "Ale", if there was a fire to "regale" or entertain their souls, they'd all "sing" like they sing in the *Songs of Innocence*, they'd never stray or leave the Church. The Little Vagabond paints an imaginary picture of how Parson might behave if he were preaching in the pub: he'd behave like someone living on *The Ecchoing Green*, he would "preach & drink & sing", and, as a result, his congregation would all be as "happy as birds in the spring". This imagery connected with birds can be found in poems such as *Spring*, *Blossom* and *The School Boy*, which deploy bird imagery to express the emotions of the characters or situations. In the next two lines we learn about "dame Lurch" who is clearly using the "birch" on the children, in other words beating them if they misbehave. If the church was more like the Ale-house she would not behave this way, nor would the children be "bandy" – bow-legged -- which indicates they are thin and unhealthy looking. Furthermore they wouldn't have to fast and go hungry. The last verse paints a picture of a different God the father to that shown in *Earth's Answer, The Garden of Love* and *The Human Abstract*; the Little Vagabond imagines him to being like a father who takes delight in seeing "His children as pleasant and happy as he". If the children were like this, he'd no longer have any disagreements with people who drink from the alcoholic "Barrel" or behave like they're the Devil because they would not be straying in the way they currently do. As a result, God would provide proper clothing for the people by giving them "apparel" and he would also give them "drink" or alcohol.

To sum up, *The Little Vagabond* paints a picture of what might be if the attitudes of the Ale-house were transposed to the church; everyone would be much happier and healthier, and more religious.

Further investigations

Some people think that Blake is celebrating the ways of the non-conformist churches here, many of which met in Ale-houses because they were banned from worshipping in churches. It is worth investigating the attitudes of the dissenting sects of Christianity in order to appreciate Blake's attitude more fully.

You can examine different versions of this poem here:

http://www.blakearchive.org/exist/blake/archive/comparison.xq?selection=compare&copies=all&bentleynum=B45&copyid=songsie.b&java=

London

Pre-reading

What are your views of big cities? Why do people live in them? What are their advantages and disadvantages? What are the problems of big cities?

> I wander thro' each charter'd street,
> Near where the charter'd Thames does flow
> And mark in every face I meet
> Marks of weakness, marks of woe.
>
> In every cry of every Man,
> In every Infants cry of fear,
> In every voice; in every ban,
> The mind-forg'd manacles I hear
>
> How the Chimney-sweepers cry
> Every blackning Church appalls,
> And the hapless Soldiers sigh
> Runs in blood down Palace walls
>
> But most thro' midnight streets I hear
> How the youthful Harlots curse
> Blasts the new born Infants tear
> And blights with plagues the Marriage hearse

Questions

What does "charter'd" mean? Why are both the streets and the Thames "charter'd"?

Why does the poet notice "marks of weakness" and "woe" in every face? Who do you think is narrating this poem?

Why does the poet "hear" "mind-forged manacles" in every cry? What does Blake mean by this phrase?

Why does the "Chimney-sweepers cry" "appal" "every blackning church"? Why might the churches be "blackning"?

Why is the sigh of the Soldier running in blood "down Palace walls"? Why is the Soldier "hapless"? What is the Palace a "metonym" for?

Why does the poet hear about the "curse" of the "youthful Harlot"? What does this curse do to new born babies and why? Why are marriages ruined by plagues? Why are marriages like "hearses"?

Creative response

Write your own poem about a nasty or very unpleasant place you know about very well. Describe the sights, the sounds and the most horrific scenes. Describe what you have seen and heard. Try not to make anything up.

Analysis

You can watch a video of me explaining this poem here: http://www.youtube.com/watch?v=vXpdh6uoiUY

The poem opens with the poet describing how he walks through each "charter'd" street near the Thames, which is also described as "charter'd". This is an adjective which has both a general and a specific meaning. During Blake's life-time "to charter" was coming to mean "to limit" or "to hire", but it was also a reference to the ancient charters which granted freedoms to the English people, with the most famous charter being the Magna Carter of 1215 which guaranteed the English their freedom. Therefore we can see that the adjective could mean two contradictory things: a "charter'd street" could be a place where you are free, or where your freedoms are limited. More recently, we could talk about "charter'd" meaning "mapped out". In a first draft Blake used the adjective "dirty". If Blake did mean that the streets were places of freedom this would almost certainly have been ironic because in the rest of the poem it is very clear that the inhabitants of London are very far from free. The poet "marks" or notices in every face how weak they look and how miserable. The repetition of the word "mark" is powerfully effective for a number of reasons: first, it gives the poem a thumping, emphatic rhythm, but second it makes us think about the different meanings of "mark". The word shifts from being a verb in line 3 to being a noun in line 4: the marks of "weakness" and of "woe" are like scars that brand the faces of the Londoners. Blake employs a similar technique to create a very different effect in the _Introduction_ to *Innocence*.

The suffering is ubiquitous, or all-pervasive (it is everywhere): Blake conveys the sense that no Londoner escapes from misery by using the adjective "every" to inform us that every man, child, person and public proclamation (ban) tells us that people are enslaved in their minds; their minds are "manacled" or chained to misery and reductive ways of thinking, which means that everyone is exploited. This is a world of "fear" and prohibitions: the word "ban" suggests not only a public pronouncement but also it describes how different forms of human activity are constantly being banned. We are in the world described in _The Garden of Love_ where "Thou Shalt Not" pervades the air. The second verse seamlessly runs onto the third verse because it is as a result of the "mind-forged manacles" that the Chimney Sweeper is crying with woe and the soldier is dying in battle. Blake's writing here is symbolic and densely packed. We are told that the cry of the Chimney Sweeper "appalls" the "blackning church"; this could mean that the cry of the chimney sweeper reveals the church as "appalling" or morally corrupt. Or it could mean that the church is or should be appalled by the treatment of the chimney sweepers.

The church is symbolically "blackning" because of its mental state of corruption; this is darkness that we saw in the _Earth's Answer_ where the Earth is immersed in the darkness of patriarchal oppression. Likewise, the Palace walls are running with blood because the Palace is a metonym (see _Analysing Language_ section) representing the monarchy as a whole; it is the monarchy which is sending young soldiers to their deaths in battle. The rhyme of "appalls" and "walls" highlights the fact that both the church and the monarchy are morally corrupt, complicit in the exploitation and deaths of young children and men.

Blake carefully structures this poem so that he leaves the most nightmarish aspects of London to the very last verse. The poet is an eye-witness to the midnight streets: this is both the literal "midnight" streets and the metaphorical ones. These are streets immersed in the darkness of "experience". The poet sees the "youthful Harlot", the child prostitute, who has a "curse" and "curses": again we see Blake play on words here. The "curse" is both the prostitute swearing and it is the "curse" of venereal disease; in those days syphilis and gonorrhea were very common diseases and deadly as well. If untreated they are passed on from mother to child. This is what we see happening in the last lines of the poem. By extrapolation, we can work out that men are sleeping with prostitutes and then passing on their infection to their wives who are then passing them to their new-born babies. This explains why the "new-born Infant's tear" is being "blasted": the baby is born with venereal disease which frequently affects baby's faces, covering them with scabs and infections. It is also brings "plagues" into a marriage because, of course, everyone can suffer from the disease. Venereal disease was fatal then; this is why marriage is a "Hearse" or a vehicle for carrying a dead body to a funeral. Equally, these lines could be interpreted more literally; the prostitute's curse is literal in that the harlot is swearing at the new born baby, "blasting" it with the force of its shouting.

 The poem ends with an apocalyptic picture of the family being killed off by the plagues of London. The powerful rhyme of "curse" and "hearse" only serves to highlight the horror of what is happening in London.

 The poem is written in an iambic metre which mimicks the footsteps of someone walking the streets of London; alliteration, repetition and rhyme is used to bring extra force to the rhythm. Blake varies the rhythm to give the poem an extra dynamism and convey a sense of horror and confusion. You could almost pick any part of the poem to show this, but let's look at the first verse. Heavy beats are highlighted in bold.

> I **wan**der **thro'** each **char**ter'd **street**,
> **Near** where the **char**ter'd **Thames** does **flow**
> And **mark** in **every** **face** I **meet**
> **Marks** of **weak**ness, **marks** of **woe**.

Notice how the first three lines are more or less totally iambic, providing a regular rhythmic pattern, which is very like the sensation of walking, but the last line of the verse is "trochaic" with the heavy beat falling on the first syllable of the line. Thus Blake reverses the rhythm at a moment when he begins to describe the depressed, sorrowful state of the people of London. The rhythm thus catches us unawares, it surprises us with its change of pace and approach, making us possibly feel the confusion and horror of the Londoners as we read the line aloud.

Further investigations

A great deal has been written about this poem so it's worth reading what different critics think of it. Even though it is one of Blake less ambiguous poems, it has its difficulties.

You see different versions of the poem here:

http://www.blakearchive.org/exist/blake/archive/comparison.xq?selection=compare&copies=all&bentleynum=B46&copyid=songsie.b&java=

You can see different versions of the poem Blake wrote of *London* in the British Library collection here:
http://www.bl.uk/onlinegallery/ttp/blake/accessible/folion113andn112.html

Francis Gilbert

The Human Abstract
Pre-reading
Why do you think poverty exists? Why are people poor? Why do people like being charitable? Is being generous always a selfless act? Why do people pretend to be "humble" and not very knowledgeable when actually they are? Why do people deceive each other?

Pity would be no more,
If we did not make somebody Poor:
And Mercy no more could be,
If all were as happy as we:

And mutual fear brings peace:
Till the selfish loves increase.
Then Cruelty knits a snare,
And spreads his baits with care.

He sits down with holy fears,
And waters the ground with tears:
Then Humility takes its root
Underneath his foot.

Soon spreads the dismal shade
Of Mystery over his head;
And the Catterpiller and Fly,
Feed on the Mystery.

And it bears the fruit of Deceit,
Ruddy and sweet to eat:
And the Raven his nest has made
In its thickest shade.

The Gods of the earth and sea,
Sought thro' Nature to find this Tree

Songs of Innocence and Experience: A Study Guide

> But their search was all in vain;
> There grows one in the Human Brain

Questions

What would stop people feeling pity in Blake's view?

What would end the idea of "mercy"?

Why does "mutual fear" bring peace?

Why do people pretend to be humble in Blake's view?

What is the Tree of Mystery and what enables it to grow? What sort creatures like to nest in the Tree of Mystery and why? What do these creatures symbolise?

Why do so many Gods and people search for the Tree of Mystery?

Why does the Tree of Mystery grow in the human brain?

Creative response

Write a series of aphorisms (short, pithy and memorable sayings) like Blake's on these topics:

Poverty

Rich people

Poor people

Keeping secrets

Pretending to be someone you are not

Religious faith

The mystery of life

The meaning of life

Analysis

You can watch a video of me explaining this poem here: http://www.youtube.com/watch?v=ea6961dcL9I

The title of the poem is important. Blake saw abstraction as the product of excessive logical thought which seeks to generalize rather than particularize, that is to say it looks to make general rules and laws that apply to all people rather than to describe a particular situation. As we have seen in *The Garden of Love* and *London*, Blake viewed many laws/rules/codes as being very destructive. The adjective "human" here means to be fallible or erroneous. So we could interpret the title as meaning "the wrong kind of abstractions or rules or laws".

He opens the poem with a striking aphorism or saying which uses rhyme to make its message memorable: "Pity would be no more/If we did not make somebody Poor". In other words, what seems to be a noble emotion is not actually noble at all because you only feel it if someone is disadvantaged or less powerful than yourself. This comment is an outright challenge to Blake's poem *The Divine Image* which celebrated "Pity" as a positive emotion which revealed mankind's essential oneness and common goodness. Likewise, Blake now deconstructs or undermines another concept celebrated in *The Divine Image*, that of "Mercy" -- which again, like Pity, only occurs when there is an emotional imbalance. It is difficult to know whether Blake is being ironic here because as we've already said he celebrates Pity and Mercy in *The Divine Image*. In *The Clod and the Pebble* he shows how a lowly Clod of Clay can exhibit unselfish emotions, even though he is far more disadvantaged than many around him.

Blake develops some of the ideas that we saw in *The Clod and the Pebble* by showing how opposing sides can find peace if they are both frightened of each other. But there is an unseen consequence to this sort of peace: "the selfish loves increase". People nurture their own selfish concerns, forgetting to consider others. They become paranoid and secretly plot to hurt other people. Blake personifies "Cruelty" as a person who "knits" or devises a "snare" or trap and carefully lays bait for people to be trapped by. The idea here is similar to that of *A Poison Tree*. People who appear to be peaceful and loving but are only being this way because they are afraid inevitably become secretive and conspiratorial; their repressed angry is channeled into plotting secretly against others. Blake is developing a theory here of "repression" which is similar to the psycho-analyst Sigmund Freud, who nearly a hundred years later, would argue that people need to express their emotions if they are to avoid mental illness.

In the third verse Blake shows how Cruelty disguises himself with "holy fears": he looks like he is religious and caring for other people by expressing his fears for their souls. He cries hypocritical tears which give the impression that he is humble or someone who doesn't think about himself. This "humility takes its root/Underneath its foot"; in other words, this false humility become a root which grows underneath him until it grows into a "Tree of Mystery" which is very similar to the nasty tree of hidden malice that Blake talks about in *A Poison Tree*. This symbol derives from the "tree of knowledge of good and evil" which Eve ate from in the Garden of Eden. We can see here Blake writing another version of the Fall – a symbolic story he describes a few times in the *Songs of Experience*. Blake hated the idea of "Mystery" because he felt that it created false hierarchies of knowledge, giving power to the people who held the secret of the mystery and disempowering those who didn't have access to the secret code. Only the "Caterpiller and Fly" – presumably unpleasant insects – benefit from eating from the Tree of Mystery; it nurtures unpleasant mentalities. The Tree bears the "fruit of Deceit" in much the same way the Poison Tree produces a poisonous fruit too. It looks very appealing but it is deadly. The Raven, a carnivorous (meat-eating) bird, can hide amidst its "thickest shade"; evil people can hide themselves in the tree.

The last verse talks about how all the Gods look for the Tree of Mystery, searching for it as a real thing which exists in the universe. They are hoping it will be an answer to all of their problems. In other words, the Gods are guilty of "false consciousness" or an approach to life which requires there to be an ultimate meaning or secret to life, but as Blake says in the last lines, there is no answer to life, there is no "Mystery" to be solved because everything originates from the "Human Brain". This is a very daring thing for Blake to say; he is effectively saying that there is no "external God", there is no answer to the riddle of human life residing in the skies, there is only what we can work out for ourselves in the Human Brain.

Further investigations
Re-read *A Poison Tree* and *The Garden of Love* and work out the similarities and differences between these poems and *The Human Abstract*.

You can find different versions of this poem here:
http://www.blakearchive.org/exist/blake/archive/comparison.xq?selection=compare&copies=all&bentleynum=B47&copyid=songsie.b&java=

Infant Sorrow

Pre-reading

Why is it so upsetting to see little children suffer? What effect do you think poverty and abusive parents have on children? How important are the early experiences of a young child on shaping the adult?

My mother groand! my father wept.
Into the dangerous world I leapt:
Helpless, naked, piping loud:
Like a fiend hid in a cloud.

Struggling in my fathers hands:
Striving against my swadling bands:
Bound and weary I thought best
To sulk upon my mothers breast.

Questions

Why does the mother groan and the father weep?

Why does the child "leap" into the world? Why is the world dangerous?

Why does the child compare himself to being "like a fiend hid in a cloud"? Discuss the implications of this simile.

How does Blake use alliteration to great effect in this poem?

Why does the child "sulk" on his mother's breast?

Creative response

Write a description of a moaning, crying, angry child or baby.

Analysis

You can watch a video of me explaining this poem here:
http://www.youtube.com/watch?v=y9CLe058D_Q

Songs of Innocence and Experience: A Study Guide

This poem is the companion poem to *Infant Joy* in the *Songs of Innocence*. It is a powerfully rhythmic poem which describes the misery of an unwanted child arriving into the world of experience. This is the "dangerous" world described in London where everyone is brainwashed into accepting a pernicious social system. As with *Infant Joy*, Blake speaks with the voice of the new-born child to begin with. The energy of the angry child is suggested by Blake's verbal choices; the child has "leapt" into the world, it is "piping loud"; it is "struggling", "striving" and it "sulks". This said, we also learn that the child soon loses its rebellious nature because it is "bound" and this makes it "weary" or tired. The rebellion is short-lived. Nevertheless, the alliterative quality of "leapt" and "loud" lend force to the angry resistance of the child, while the sibilance of "struggling", "striving" and "sulk" give the child a sinister, serpent-like quality. The fact that the child is "piping" recalls the Piper of the *Songs of Innocence*; like the Piper he is wild, but he has no outlet for his imagination, no chance to roam free and no opportunities to enjoy the songs of happy "chear". Instead he is imprisoned or "bound" by the hands of his father and his "swaddling bands". The alliteration of "bands" "bound" "best" and "breast" serve to underline the imprisonment of the child. The poem uses rhyming couplets to add emphasis to its fundamental message: the world of experience is no place for a child to be born into. It is a place which robs children of their humanity.

Further investigations

You can find different versions of this poem here:
http://www.blakearchive.org/exist/blake/archive/comparison.xq?selection=compare&copies=all&bentleynum=B48&copyid=songsie.b&java=

This academic website provides various sources for *Infant Sorrow*:
http://www.english.uga.edu/wblake/SONGS/48/48bib.html

You can look at Blake's notebook on the British Library website here, which shows a longer version he wrote of the poem:
http://www.bl.uk/onlinegallery/ttp/blake/accessible/folion113andn112.html

Francis Gilbert

A Poison Tree

Pre-reading

When and why do people pretend to be nice to each other when really they hate each other?

I was angry with my friend:
I told my wrath, my wrath did end.
I was angry with my foe:
I told it not, my wrath did grow.

And I waterd it in fears,
Night & morning with my tears:
And I sunned it with smiles,
And with soft deceitful wiles.

And it grew both day and night,
Till it bore an apple bright.
And my foe beheld it shine,
And he knew that it was mine.

And into my garden stole,
When the night had veild the pole;
In the morning glad I see,
My foe outstretchd beneath the tree.

Questions

Why does the poet's anger with his friend disappear?
Why does the poet's anger with his enemy grow?
What form does his hidden anger grow into?
How and why does the poet deceive his enemy?
What does the Poison Tree represent or symbolize?
How does Blake use rhythm and rhyme to create interest and drama in this poem?

Analysis

Songs of Innocence and Experience: A Study Guide

You can watch a video of me explaining and performing this poem here:
http://www.youtube.com/watch?v=2VtHjz6dREY

This poem is possibly the most effective poem Blake wrote which explores the theme of repression. Like *The Clod and the Pebble*, the "Flower" poems in *Experience*, and *The Angel* it has a fable-like quality which succinctly tells the story of how the poet harbours a secret anger or "wrath" against a "foe" or enemy which grows into a Poison Tree which looks inviting and delicious but is, in fact, poisonous. Developing ideas discussed in *The Human Abstract*, Blake describes how and why a "Tree of Mystery" comes into existence.

The poem opens by describing how the poet feels he can reveal his "anger" to his friend and as a result, his anger comes to an end. Here we see Blake showing the importance of talking through problems rather than repressing them. However, the poet does not tell his foe that he is angry with him and, as a result, the anger grows, with him watering it with "fears"; this is an image we found in *The Human Abstract*. The rhyme of "foe" and "grow" emphasize the terror of the anger growing, while the rhyme of "fears" and "tears" shows how both pity and fear are linked. The poet appears to be nice to his enemy by smiling at him but his surface appearance of being nice is merely "soft deceitful wiles": he is deceiving his enemy with "wiles" or cunning tricks. His anger grows into a tree which produces like the Tree of Knowledge in the Garden of Eden an "apple bright". The foe, believing the fruit to be good, "steals" into the poet's garden; here we see how the foe himself believes he is deceiving the poet. Clearly, he too has been "playing the game" of appearing to be nice as well. He pays for this because he never escapes from the poet's garden and is left at the end of the poem "outstretched beneath the tree"; he has died and his and the poet's trickery has been uncovered in a tragic fashion. Once again we find Blake telling another version of the Fall: the poet, who begins the poem in an "innocent" state, enters the world of experience when he represses his emotions and tricks his enemy.

Francis Gilbert

The poem uses rhyming couplets to tell its story rather like a traditional ballad. The poem contains Biblical imagery which has been developed and re-interpreted by Blake.

Further investigations

You can find different versions of the poem here:

http://www.blakearchive.org/exist/blake/archive/comparison.xq?selection=compare&copies=all&bentleynum=B49&copyid=songsie.b&java=

It is worth re-reading The Garden of Eden story in order to make connections with this poem. You should also look at *The Human Abstract* to make comparisons between this poem and it.

A Little Boy Lost (Experience)

Pre-reading

When and why do adults get angry with children? How aware are children of social conventions? How do children respond to very strict rules? Do you think it's important to be very strict with children or not?

> Nought loves another as itself
> Nor venerates another so,
> Nor is it possible to Thought
> A greater than itself to know:
>
> And Father, how can I love you,
> Or any of my brothers more?
> I love you like the little bird
> That picks up crumbs around the door.
>
> The Priest sat by and heard the child,
> In trembling zeal he siez'd his hair:
> He led him by his little coat:
> And all admir'd the Priestly care.
>
> And standing on the altar high,

Songs of Innocence and Experience: A Study Guide

Lo what a fiend is here! said he:
One who sets reason up for judge
Of our most holy Mystery.

The weeping child could not be heard,
The weeping parents wept in vain:
They strip'd him to his little shirt,
And bound him in an iron chain.

And burn'd him in a holy place,
Where many had been burn'd before:
The weeping parents wept in vain.
Are such things done on Albions shore

Questions

How and why does the little boy shock the adults around him?
   Why does the Priest become so angry?
   Why is the child a "fiend" in the Priest's view?
   Why does everyone admire the Priest?
   What is the child guilty of?
   Why is the little boy burned? Do you think it's a literal burning or a metaphorical/symbolical one?
   Witches were burned at the stake in England. Why were such things done in England?

Analysis

You can watch a video of me explaining and performing this poem here:
http://www.youtube.com/watch?v=ILFgqjiOZOU

The little boy speaking this poem opens the poem by saying a "heretical thought". According to St. Anselm, "God is the greatest thought it is possible to think" and so to say that no one loves anyone else or respects them like they respect themselves, or to say that there is no greater process of thought than finding out about your own mind is actually a "heresy". The boy asks his father how he can love him or his brothers any more than he already does. His love for them is motivated by selfishness; he loves them for the "crumbs" they can give to him in the same way a bird is appreciative of the crumbs given to it. The Priest, who hears this, immediately recognizes it as a heresy; he grabs the boy by the hair and everyone admires the Priest for "taking care" of the child, taking him in hand and disciplining him. The Priest stands on the altar and calls the boy a "fiend" or devil because he has applied the logic of reason to the workings of God. The child and his family are in shock and weep, but it is "in vain" because the child is imprisoned in an "iron chain". The rhyme of "vain" and "chain" emphasizes the powerlessness of the child and family in this situation as the full force of the church is brought to bear in the child's punishment. They burn the child as a heretic, as many heretics have been burnt. The poem ends with the question as to whether such things are still done on "Albion's shore" or in England.

Although the burning of heretics had stopped by the time Blake was alive, the church and the authorities would still burn books. Thomas Paine's *The Rights of Man* was burned publicly for being heretical; Blake would have known about this because he was friendly with Paine's publisher (p. 56, Johnson and Grant).

Further investigations

In his annotations to his 1971 edition of Blake's poems, W. H. Stevenson recalls Watt's hymn On Obedience to Parents: "Have yet no heard what dreadful plagues/Are threatened by the Lord/To him that breaks his father's word?/What heavy guilt upon him lis,/How cursed is his name!/The ravens shall pick out his eyes/And eagles eat the same." How might Watt's hymn inform our reading of the poem?

You can find different versions of the poem here:

http://www.blakearchive.org/exist/blake/archive/comparison.xq?selection=compare&copies=all&bentleynum=B50&copyid=songsie.b&java=

This poem is particularly good to compare with other texts which explore the horrors of fundamentalism such Margaret Atwood's *The Handmaid's Tale*.

A Little Girl Lost (Second poem in Experience)

Pre-reading
What is special and dangerous about teenagers falling in love? Why do parents get so worried about their children's first relationships? Do you think parents over-react?

Children of the future Age,
Reading this indignant page;
Know that in a former time,
Love! sweet Love! was thought a crime.

In the Age of Gold,
Free from winters cold:
Youth and maiden bright,
To the holy light,
Naked in the sunny beams delight.

Once a youthful pair
Fill'd with softest care:
Met in garden bright,
Where the holy light,
Had just removd the curtains of the night.

There in rising day,
On the grass they play:
Parents were afar:
Strangers came not near:
And the maiden soon forgot her fear.

Tired with kisses sweet
They agree to meet,
When the silent sleep
Waves o'er heavens deep;

Francis Gilbert

And the weary tired wanderers weep.

To her father white
Came the maiden bright:
But his loving look,
Like the holy book,
All her tender limbs with terror shook.

Ona! pale and weak!
To thy father speak:
O the trembling fear!
O the dismal care!
That shakes the blossoms of my hoary hair

Questions

Blake addresses the future ages in this poem. Do you think we have changed our attitudes towards sex and relationships today from what it used to be like in Blake's time?

What does the maiden do in this poem? Why are the kisses "sweet" for them?

Why is the father so upset in the last verse of the poem?

Creative response

Write your own poem, description or story about a love affair which is forbidden and what happens when someone finds out.

Analysis

You can watch a video of me explaining this poem here: http://www.youtube.com/watch?v=X4P1g2u8s9o

Here we find Blake addresses those living now, who are "Children of the future Age". In the voice of the Bard, or poet, he tells us that there was once a time when "love" was once thought a crime. The first four verses describe an idyllic world, in the "Golden Age", when two lovers meet. The maiden "forgot her fear" and makes love to her lover. Having finished making love, they agree to meet later on during the night time when they can't be seen. When the maiden returns to her father she is frightened by his "loving look" and "All her tender limbs with terror shook".

Quite why she is frightened is not that clear. Is she frightened because her father has viewed her in a sexual way? Or is she scared because she does not want to tell her father about her lover? The father implores in the last verse to speak to her but we are not told her answer.

Further investigations

Blake is keen in much of his poetry to describe the Golden Age. In A Vision of the Lsat Judgment Blake declared that all his work is "an Endeavour to Restore the Golden Age".

You can see different versions of this poem here:

http://www.blakearchive.org/exist/blake/archive/comparison.xq?selection=compare&copies=all&bentleynum=B51&copyid=songsie.b&java=

To Tirzah

Pre-reading

How did the earth come into being? Why are there two different sexes?

Whate'er is Born of Mortal Birth,
Must be consumed with the Earth
To rise from Generation free:
Then what have I to do with thee?

The sexes sprung from Shame & Pride
Blowd in the morn; in evening died
But Mercy changd Death into Sleep;
The Sexes rose to work & weep.

Thou Mother of my Mortal part,
With cruelty didst mould my Heart.
And with false self-decieving tears,
Didst bind my Nostrils Eyes & Ears.

Didst close my Tongue in senseless clay
And me to Mortal Life betray:
The Death of Jesus set me free.
Them what have I to do with thee?

Questions

What does Blake think happens to people when they die?

How did the different sexes come into being according to Blake in verse two? What happened as a consequence of the sexes being separated into male and female?

Why was the mother of human beings cruel?

Why and how did she try and silence the poet?

Why was the poet set free by Jesus?

Why does the poet ask the question in the final line?

Creative response

Write your own creation myth explaining how the different sexes came into being and the consequences of the sexes emerging.

Analysis

You can watch a video of me explaining this poem here: http://www.youtube.com/watch?v=TJoy7VjCLlM

This is a difficult poem, full of references to Blake's own personal mythology which makes it problematic to understand. The first verse describes that whatever is born of "Mortal Birth", in other words born human, must return to the earth when it dies, and will then free itself from "Generation" or the world of experience. This fact of death means you could see yourself as entirely isolated from other people because you die alone, no one else can die your death for you. Johnson and Grant feel that the "crucial text is Jesus' rebuke of Mary just before conducting the miracle of Cana in his own way and time (John 2:4)" (p. 58).

The second verse explores Blake's own interpretation of the Creation story. He describes how the two different "Sexes", male and female, arose from "Shame and Pride". In the non-conformist Christian tradition, there was a belief, derived from the philosopher Plato, that once mankind was "androgynous" or both male and female and mankind "fell" when he was split into the different sexes of male and female. They "blowed" or spoke/communicated/existed in the morning, and then died in the evening. But Mercy ironically changed their deaths into a form of sleep and they "rose to work & weep"; thus creating an endless cycle of misery for mankind.

In the last two verses, the poet addresses the Earth Mother who created the "Mortal part" of mankind. She imprisoned the five senses of mankind by using the trickery of "false self-deceiving tears" to a world of death and senseless clay; she made people believe that they were limited by the world of the senses and that there is no spiritual existence beyond the physical world. However, the death of Jesus made the poet see that there is a life of freedom beyond the world of the senses. In his poem *The Everlasting Gospel* Blake writes about how Jesus sets people free not because he atoned for our sins but because he inspires us through his example, like the Clod of Clay, Jesus loves other people more than himself and is willing die for other people's sake.

The poet ends the poem by questioning what he is doing engaging with the Earth Mother who tricked in him into believing that there is no spiritual existence beyond the world of the senses.

It's a difficult, ambiguous poem which is really Blake's attempt at a creation myth, a re-write of the Fall.

Further investigations

This poem was added to later copies of *The Songs of Experience*. The woman Tirzah is talked about in Numbers 27:1-11, 36:3, Joshua 17:3-4, and Song of Solomon 6:4, the city of Tirzah was the capital of the Hebrew Northern Kingdom, as opposed to Jerusalem in the South. In some of Blake's other books, *The Four Zoas* VIII, *Milton* 17:11, and *Jerusalem* 67, 68, Tirzah and her cohort Rahab engage in sexual tortures of the male (p. 58, Johnson and Grant).

The inscription that accompanies the poem on the plate, "It is Raised a spiritual body", is from I Corinthians 15:44. The whole passage beginning at Chapter 15: 35 was of the greatest interest to Blake who uses it in many places in his poetry.

You can find a version of the poem here:

Francis Gilbert

http://www.blakearchive.org/exist/blake/archive/object.xq?objectid=songsie.l.illbk.42&java=no

The School Boy

Pre-reading

What is your attitude towards school? Do you really think it has helped you develop as a person? Would you have learnt more by not going to school? What are the advantages and disadvantages of school?

I love to rise in a summer morn,
When the birds sing on every tree;
The distant huntsman winds his horn,
And the sky-lark sings with me.
O! what sweet company.

But to go to school in a summer morn,
O! it drives all joy away;
Under a cruel eye outworn,
The little ones spend the day,
In sighing and dismay.

Ah! then at times I drooping sit,
And spend many an anxious hour,
Nor in my book can I take delight,
Nor sit in learnings bower,
Worn thro' with the dreary shower.

How can the bird that is born for joy,
Sit in a cage and sing.
How can a child when fears annoy,
But droop his tender wing,
And forget his youthful spring.

O! father & mother, if buds are nip'd,

Songs of Innocence and Experience: A Study Guide

> And blossoms blown away,
> And if the tender plants are strip'd
> Of their joy in the springing day,
> By sorrow and cares dismay,
>
> How shall the summer arise in joy
> Or the summer fruits appear.
> Or how shall we gather what griefs destroy
> Or bless the mellowing year,
> When the blasts of winter appear.

Questions

What does the school-boy love to do?

Why does the school-boy not enjoy school? Find three reasons why he doesn't like it, providing quotation to back up your points.

Why does the school-boy compare children to birds in a cage and buds that are "nip'd"?

What does the school-boy see might be a consequence of the restrictive schooling children have received in the final verse?

Creative response

Write your own poem about school, describing its sights, sounds, smells and tastes. It could more or less negative than Blake's poem.

Analysis

You can watch my explanation and performance of this poem here:

http://www.youtube.com/watch?v=dCEvoTMNnww

Once again, we have Blake describing another version of the Fall. Spoken in the voice of a school boy he talks about the boy's love of the "summer morn", his delight in hearing the "birds sing on every tree" and the "huntsman winds his horn". Nature is at one with the boy as the "sky-lark sings with me". We are once again in the world of *Innocence*, similar to that evoked in *The Ecchoing Green*, *Spring*, *The Shepherd* and *The Lamb*. For this reason, it is not hard to see that originally Blake placed this poem in the *Songs of Innocence* collection.

The second verse though takes us into the world of experience; the joy of the boy is driven away. The "cruel eye" of the teacher watches over him, while the other pupils spend their days "In sighing and dismay". The boy is described as "drooping" and feeling "anxious". He is metaphorically subjected to a "dreary shower" of words and is not able to "sit in learnings bower". The imagery here suggests that learning can be flourishing and natural thing like a "bower" or lovely shady place is. The school boy compares himself to a bird trapped in a cage and has lost his natural desire to sing, whose "tender wing" now droops, and who loses his "youthful spring". The penultimate verse compares the students to buds which are "nip'd/And blossoms blown away" or "tender plants" that are "strip'd/Of their joy" when they really shouldn't be. They are afflicted with "sorrow", "cares" and "dismay". As a result, the boy wonders what will happen when these children grow up; will the "summer fruit appear"? Will the next generation be able to innovate, to be creative, to think for themselves? How will they cope, having been stripped of their humanity, when "the blasts of winter appear"?

We have here an explanation of how the "manacles" of the mind are "forged", an image which Blake used in London. He shows here how the delight and wonder is stripped from the students and instead they are forced like birds to be in cages.

Further investigations

You can find different versions of the poem here:

http://www.blakearchive.org/exist/blake/archive/comparison.xq?selection=compare&copies=all&bentleynum=B53&copyid=songsie.b&java=

Do some research into what school was like in Blake's time and consider the psychological effects of children going to schools they don't like.

The Voice of the Ancient Bard

Pre-reading

When have you felt real hope in your life? At what times of the day and year do you feel hope? Why do people feel hope? Why are people inclined to follow and believe in people who talk in a hopeful fashion? Why do people follow leaders who don't know what they're talking about and ignore the advice of wise people?

> Youth of delight come hither,
> And see the opening morn,
> Image of truth new born.
> Doubt is fled & clouds of reason,
> Dark disputes & artful teazing.
> Folly is an endless maze.
> Tangled roots perplex her ways,
> How many have fallen there!
> They stumble all night over bones of the dead:
> And feel they know not what but care:
> And wish to lead others when they should be led

Questions

Why is the youth someone who feels "delight"?
Why does the poet call the youth to come to him?
Why is a new truth being born?
Why has doubt disappeared?
How and why do people lose their way in life according to the last half of the poem? Explain some of the imagery in this section, discussing what "tangled roots" and the "bones of the dead" might symbolize.

Creative response

Write a very hopeful poem which suggests that all the problems of the world might soon be solved.

Analysis

You can watch me explain and perform this poem here:
http://www.youtube.com/watch?v=ob_cHXo5x8E

Francis Gilbert

This poem was once in the *Songs of Innocence* but was transferred to the end of the *Songs of Experience* possibly so that the collection ends on a positive note and provides symmetry to the collection: remember that the *Songs of Experience* begins with the *Introduction* which tells us to listen to the voice of the Bard, or the holy Poet. The Bard here asks the Youth of delight to come to him; this is presumably someone like the School Boy or the lovers in *A Little Girl Lost*. The Bard says that a new truth has come upon the earth; there is no more "doubt" because it has "fled" as has "dark disputes & artful teasing". The sorts of destructive behavior we witnessed in *A Poison Tree* or *The Human Abstract* has disappeared. These people who feed off the "Tree of Mystery" are endlessly caught upon in "folly" or foolishness. They have fallen over the roots of the Tree of Mystery like many other people, and they spend their time in a permanent night, stumbling over the useless bones of the dead. They are full of "care" or worry, and yet want to lead other people down the same dark path, even though they themselves should be led by more enlightened people.

Further investigations

You can see different versions of this poem here:

http://www.blakearchive.org/exist/blake/archive/comparison.xq?selection=compare&copies=all&bentleynum=B54&copyid=songsie.b&java=

Compare this poem with the poems that begin and end both books, and think about why Blake has decided upon these poems to begin and end his collections.

A Divine Image (Experience)

Pre-reading

Why are people cruel to each other? Why do they feel jealousy? Why do people terrorise each other? Why do people keep secrets from each other?

> CRUELTY has a human heart,
> And Jealousy a human face;

Songs of Innocence and Experience: A Study Guide

> Terror the human form divine,
> And Secrecy the human dress.
>
> The human dress is forgèd iron,
> The human form a fiery forge,
> The human face a furnace seal'd,
> The human heart its hungry gorge.

Questions

This poem was originally a draft of *The Human Abstract* but was left out of the *Songs of Experience* after Blake wrote *The Human Abstract*. Why do you think he did this?

Why does Blake feel that all these concepts are "human"? What is Blake saying about humanity here?

What is the "human dress"? Why might it be forged in iron?

Why is the face like a "furnace"?

Why is the heart like a "hungry gorge"?

Compare this poem with *The Divine Image*. What are the similarities and differences between the two poems?

Creative response

Write your own poem, essay or article about why cruelty, jealousy, terror and secrecy exist. Or write an allegory about these things turning each concept into a person, e.g. describe/personify cruelty, jealousy, terror, and secrecy.

Analysis

This poem was engraved for the *Songs of Experience*, but then replaced by *The Human Abstract*. It reverses many of the points of *The Divine Image* in the *Songs of Innocence* revealing Blake's anger at the ways in which human beings can be jealous, cruel, secretive and terrifying. It seems to provide a bitterly ironic contrast to *The Divine Image* without fully explaining its points; this is possibly why Blake replaced it with the more thought-through and intellectual *The Human Abstract*.

Further investigations

Compare this poem with *The Divine Image* and *The Human Abstract*.

How to do well when writing about Blake's poetry

Read the poems, re-read them, and then re-read them again. Sing them, set them to music!

Read the critics on Blake's poetry: read annotations to his poetry, read my study guide, other study guides, and other relevant critics.

Discuss him with other students, with your teacher, and pose questions about his poetry: look at my introduction if you are stuck for questions to ask.

Read a biography of Blake: Bedard – a short biography -- and Ackroyd – a longer biography -- are the best.

Make good notes on the poems.

Draw out the common themes, ideas, imagery, poetic techniques.

Learn about how Blake uses rhythm and rhyme.

Discuss Blake with friends, family and teachers.

Be enthusiastic: see the positives in studying him.

Respond creatively to him; write your own poems in response to his poems, draw pictures inspired by his ones.

Find the poem which goes with the "contextual" quote or comment.

This exercise requires you to look at the following quotes or points and try and think about what poem or poems are relevant to it. In the process, you will be thinking about the contexts that Blake's poetry arose from because you will be trying to relate this sort of contextual information to his poetry. Remember there is no right or wrong answer, but I have followed this section with my suggestions.

Songs of Innocence and Experience: A Study Guide

The Greek God Pan is associated with playing a pipe in the countryside, with conducting parties, with playing with nymphs; with drinking and singing and poetry.

Possible answer: *Introductions* to *Songs of Innocence & Experience.*

John 10:11: "I am the good shepherd: the good shepherd giveth his life for the sheep"; Psalms 23:1-6 (A Psalm of David.) "The LORD is my shepherd; I shall not want"; John, 1.36 "The next day, John seeth Jesus coming unto him, and said, Behold the Lamb of God, which taketh away the sin of the world."

Possible answers: *The Shepherd & The Lamb*

Slavery was abolished in 1833 and generated huge wealth for merchants during Blake's lifetime. Blake wrote the *Songs of Innocence and Experience* between 1789-94.

Possible answer: *The Little Black Boy*

The Romantic poets led a movement to celebrate nature and natural environments; they felt that nature embodied the human imagination.

Possible answers: *The Blossom, Spring*

During Blake's lifetime, at the age of four and five, boys were sold to clean chimneys, due to their small size.

Possible answer: *The Chimney Sweeper*

In London, even by 1760, almost a decade and a half after the level of infant and child mortality had begun to fall, 49% of all children were dead by the age of two, and 60% by the age of five. Blake himself, one of a family of four, was born two years after the death of his infant brother, John. Possible answer: The Lost Children poems: *The Little Boy Lost, A Little Girl Lost* etc; *Infant Sorrow.*

This is a verse from Dr. Watt's *Cradle Hymn* (1674-1748): "HUSH, my dear; lie still and slumber/Holy angels guard thy bed;/Heavenly blessings, without number,/Gently falling on thy head."

Possible answer: *A Cradle Song*

William Blake's childhood home in Soho was next to a workhouse where young orphans were brought up. They were taken to Wimbledon Common by "Nurses", or nannies, who were hired by the workhouse to supervise them. They would play in the fresh air there. Later on, this practice was stopped, and the children were kept in the workhouse most of the time. (Bedard, Crehan)

Possible answer: *The Nurse's Song*

It is a heresy (against the law of the church) to say that all religions are the same, and that the human brain is where God lives.

Possible answer: *The Divine Image*

During Blake's time, England was emerging as a world empire, and was engaged in various wars and conflicts with other countries. Its chief enemy was France, which had had a revolution from 1789-99 and abolished its monarchy. Some people viewed the animal of the tiger as a symbol for the French revolution because it was an angry, devastating animal. Blake was very sympathetic towards the French revolution before it became very violent. He wrote a number of other poems which explored the horrors of the British empire. (Crehan)

Possible answer: *London*

Once a year, beginning in 1782, as many as 6,000 homeless children were marched from their charity schools all over London to attend services held in St Pauls' Cathedral. This spectacle in honour of the patrons and founders of the schools took place on a Thursday. (Johnson and Grant, p. 32)

Possible answer: *Holy Thursday*

King Lear Act IV, sc 1, l. 36-37: "As flies to wanton boys are we to the gods/They kill us for their sport."

Possible answer: *The Fly*

Many dissenting sects (factions of the Christian religion which were often banned by official Christianity) held their meetings in ale houses and pubs during Blake's life-time because they weren't allowed to worship in church.

Possible answer: *The Little Vagabond.*

Many years after Blake died, Sigmund Freud developed a theory about "repression" in which he argued that if people did not talk about their emotions, particularly anger and sexual attraction, they would become "neurotic" or mentally ill and do things that were harmful to themselves and other people without knowing why they had done them. This was because they had "repressed" their emotions. He also argued that many of their secret desires would emerge in their dreams.

Possible answer: *A Dream, The Angel, A Poison Tree.*

The figure of the Bard, or the travelling poet, is a powerful one in early English mythology; it is believed he was a wise man who people listened to. Artists and poets were, though, in Blake's lifetime, viewed with considerable suspicion and sometimes arrested for their beliefs. Blake himself was put on trial for sedition, being accused of criticising the king, but was acquitted. The experience was very traumatic for Blake.

Possible answer: *The Voice of the Ancient Bard.*

The Biblical prophet Isaiah wrote about "the wolf dwelling with the lamb while the leopard lies down with the kid… and the young lion" (Isaiah 11:6).

Possible answer: *Night.*

In his epic poem about the Fall of Man, *Paradise Lost* Book 1, 254-55, John Milton wrote: "The Mind is its own place, and in itself/Can make a Heaven of Hell, a Hell of Heaven."

Possible answer: *The Clod and the Pebble.*

Common themes in Blake's poetry

Innocence & Experience. These are obviously the main themes that Blake explores. As he states on his title page, he is aiming to explore the "Contraries" of the human soul. These are some key questions to consider when exploring his themes: what animals, plants, people and things symbolise innocence for Blake and why? What concepts, people, plants and objects symbolise experience for Blake and why? What sorts of attitudes, beliefs and ways of being do innocent people have, according to Blake? What sorts of attitudes and approaches to life do "experienced" people take?

Religion. The Christian religion dominates this collection: the Bible provides much imagery which informs the poems.

City and country. The countryside and the city are represented in very different ways. What imagery and atmospheres are associated with the countryside and the city?

The imagination. Blake places great importance upon the imagination. When and why does he do this?

Reason/logic. Blake depicts reason in a very negative light in his poetry. When and why does he do this?

Patriarchy. Much of the time powerful men are revealed in a negative light. When and why does Blake do this?

Repression. Blake reveals the dangers of people repressing their emotions. When and why does Blake do this?

Rules and regulations: codification. Blake reveals the deployment of rules and regulations as being oppressive and the lack of them as being a positive thing. When and why does he do this?

Comparing Blake with other texts

It is often a requirement for Blake to be compared with other texts. It is worthwhile going through these steps if you are going to come up with a creditable essay.

First step. Work out what the common themes, images and techniques are. Brainstorm and make notes on these.

Second step. Find key quotes which reveal links between the texts.

Third step. Have a go at structuring and planning your essays in rough.

Four step. Write a rough draft of your essay.

Fifth step. Read your essay aloud to a partner, discussing what is good about your essay and what could be improved.

Sixth step. Hand in essay.

Seventh step. Get your essay back marked and really listen to the feedback you have got from your teacher; have a go at a re-draft and see if you have improved your work.

Questions to help you compare the poems

In this section, I list poems that are linked in some way and suggest questions that might help you make comparisons between them.

The *Introductions* to the *Songs of Innocence* and *Experience*: *Earth's Answer, The Voice of Ancient Bard*. How are the figures of the Piper and the Bard similar and different in these poems? Why do a "child on a cloud" and the "Holy Word" appear in these poems? Do you think they are connected in some kind of way? If so, why? The first *Introduction* is written like a nursery rhyme, while the other *Introduction* and *Earth's Answer* are structured in a more unorthodox way. Why is this do you think? All three poems are about people being "called" to do things. What are these things that they are "called" to do and why have they been "called" to do them? How do these poems use rhythm and rhyme to create tension and draw attention to key ideas, feelings and images?

The Shepherd, The Lamb, Night, The Chimney Sweeper (Innocence), The Little Black Boy, The Tyger. All of these poems make reference to lambs: how and why? Is there a common theme here?

Spring, Blossom, Introduction to Innocence, The Ecchoing Green, Night, Earth's Answer, The Nurse's Songs. How does Blake depict nature in these poems? How does he use rhythm and rhyme to achieve his effects?

The Shepherd, The Garden of Love and the *Nurse's Songs* (both *Innocence* and *Experience*). The figure of the "Guardian" or parent is very important in these poems. How does Blake reveal two very different parenting styles? What is Blake saying about being a guardian or parent in these poems?

The Ecchoing Green and *The Garden of Love*. How are the societies that Blake depicts here similar and different? What has happened to the world of *The Ecchoing Green* in *The Garden of Love*? Why has it been destroyed? How does he use rhythm and rhyme to achieve his effects?

The Little Black Boy, The Chimney Sweeper poems (Innocence and Experience) and The Little Vagabond. In what ways do these poems present children? Why and how are they presented as victims? How does he use rhythm and rhyme to achieve his effects?

Infant Joy and Infant Sorrow, London, The Chimney Sweeper poems (Innocence and *Experience) The School Boy.* How are these poems similar and different in their depiction of young children and the world they are born into? What is Blake saying about education in these poems? How does he use rhythm and rhyme to achieve his effects?

The Little Boy Lost and The Little Boy Found (Innocence) A Little Boy Lost, The Little Girl Lost, The Little Girl Found, A Little Girl Lost (Experience). What similar experiences do all these lost children suffer in the poems? In what ways do the parents behave in these poems? What role does religion, religious imagery and religious authority play in the poems? How is the world of *Experience* different from that of *Innocence*? How is the use of rhythm and rhyme similar and different in the poems? Why do you think Blake kept returning to this story again and again?

The Nurse's Song (Innocence), Laughing Song, The Chimney Sweeper (Experience), The Nurse's song (Experience). These poems explore different emotional states of children and adults. What states do these explore and represent, and why? How does he use rhythm and rhyme to achieve his effects?

The Divine Image, Another's Sorrow, The Human Abstract, The Clod and the Pebble and The Poison Tree. All three of these poems explore the ways in which individuals affect the world around them. How and why do they do this? How does he use rhythm and rhyme to achieve his effects?

Holy Thursday (Innocence and Experience), London, The

Garden of Love and The Chimney Sweeper poems. These poems look at the treatment of children by the religious authorities. What is Blake saying about religious authority in these poems? How does he use poetic techniques to achieve his purposes? How does he use rhythm and rhyme to achieve his effects?

The Lamb, The Tyger, The Fly. What is Blake saying about animals in these poems? How and why does he use them as literary devices? How does he use rhythm and rhyme to achieve his effects?

A Dream, The Chimney Sweeper (Innocence), The Angel. What role do dreams play in Blake's poems? Why are they so important do you think? How does he use rhythm and rhyme to achieve his effects?

How to write a good essay on Blake

If you are going to do well when writing about Blake, you will need to know his work well, and to read widely about his writing. There is no magic formula to gaining a top grade. English is quite unlike many other subjects in that it requires original thought and personal response. The best answers will surprise an examiner while answering the question as well. These essays will contain an overview of Blake's poetry, but also will focus upon analysing his poetry closely; it is this combination of having a confident overview and close textual analysis which is usually what attains the best results. This said, sometimes wonderful answers can stray from this well-established approach. The point is you can't prescribe precisely what makes a top grade answer -- that's the whole point!

Nevertheless, I'm going to "stick my neck out". I am going to model to you how you might respond to this question and in the process talk about how you might write a good essay:

Francis Gilbert

How does Blake represent the worlds of innocence and experience in his poetry?

The first thing you need to do is to plan out your possible response by brainstorming your thoughts. If you feel that you are not that familiar with the poetry, you will need to re-read it; this may be a good idea anyway, even if you feel confident that you know his poetry; re-reading a writer's work is never going to hinder your progress. When planning out a response, write down all your thoughts and then order them. For example, you could write something like this, which is fairly random:

> Contraries of the human soul
> *The Lamb*, *The Shepherd*, the infant & children generally, *The Chimney Sweeper*, *The Little Black Boy*, *The Blossom*, the kind Nurse are representative of innocence; think about their shared qualities
> *The Ecchoing Green*, *Spring*, *Night* are places where innocence exists either in time or space, or both
> *The Tyger*, the jealous Nurse, *The Sick Rose*, *The Little Vagabond*, the inhabitants of London, the man who grows the Poison Tree, the selfish Pebble, the Priests in their black gowns are all citizens of the world of experience
> The Chapel on the green, London, the Tree of Mystery, the school, the howling storm, the wintery land are all places of experience
> Blake's descriptions are diverse and intellectually challenging; while some representations of the world of innocence and experience are straightforward, many are complex.
> HOW? Blake uses the form of poetry, the short lyric, and the illuminated book to represent these worlds; the arts are woven together. Concentrate upon his use of poetic form; often using familiar

Songs of Innocence and Experience: A Study Guide

poetic forms such as the ballad, the hymn, the lullaby and changing them beyond recognition.

After putting down all your thoughts, you will need to order them into some coherent, logical form so that you build up an argument.

INTRODUCTION: introduce the topics of innocence and experience and how Blake could have represented them,
MAIN BODY: look at how Blake represents the citizens, the creatures, the beings of the world of innocence, and how he invites the reader to draw contrasts in Songs of Experience
MAIN BODY: look at how Blake paints a picture of particular places
CONCLUSION: Sum up main findings.

Do you see how having brainstormed all my notes, I have decided to focus upon two main areas in my essay? I have decided to talk about the "beings" in Blake's world, and then the places, focusing upon his techniques when discussing them. Remember this question is about HOW he represents this world; that means I will have to discuss his techniques because it is by examining the ways in which he uses various techniques to bring these worlds to life in literature that I will be discussing HOW he does what he does.

So, having read the poems, written a plan, and then structured it, I am ready to start writing the essay. Lots of students I talk to really struggle over introductions. My advice is to start with a quote. I know that many teachers may tell you not to do this -- it is not the "traditional" way to start an essay -- but I like to do it because it keeps my focus upon the text and gives me a starting point. Too many students write conclusions for their introductions, telling the reader what they are going to discover in their essay. This is a real problem because a) why read the rest of the essay if you already know the answer? b) what happens if you don't show your points to be true? This often occurs with students' essays; they say will discover such and such points, and then never

181

do. It is far better to start with specific points in an introduction which address the question and then build up an argument. If you are writing a good essay, you will discover points as you write it, you will surprise yourself and the reader. The essay is a place of discovery. So here goes, I am going to start with a quotation:

> "And priests in black gowns were walking their rounds,
>   And binding with briars my joys and desires."
> William Blake's short lyric *The Garden of Love* is situated in the middle of his book, *Songs of Experience*, and is instructive in many ways.

This opening sentence is typical of the way I start essays, notice how I keep my options open; I suggest there are many points to be drawn from *The Garden of Love*. This is a good thing to do because it allows you room and space to explore points. Weaker essays tend to say that there is one point to be made when looking at a particular poem. This is the next part:

> Blake paints a picture of the ways in which the world of "experience" has corrupted an innocent world in this poem; using a first person narrator, who feels very close to the poet himself, he describes how he has gone to *The Garden of Love* and witnessed a shocking sight: there is a chapel occupying the green and 'Thou shalt not' has been written on its door. Moreover, graves have filled the beautiful space, which used to have flowers.

Notice here how I have contextualised my quote; I have explained the poem clearly, mostly in my own words, and I am now ready to start looking in depth at the language in my quotation. It is important to contextualise your quotation because otherwise the reader can become bewildered as to what is going on. This the next section:

Songs of Innocence and Experience: A Study Guide

> Blake has used the form of the ballad to deliver his points; this leads the reader to think that there will be a fleshed-out story with a clear beginning, middle and end, but what is surprising about this poem is that there is no "proper" ending. It stops just where many poems would continue. We are told that "priests in black gowns" are patrolling in "rounds"; this suggests that they are like policemen or soldiers, keeping the people of the green in order. The last line tells us what they are doing: they are "binding with briars" the "joys and desires" of the narrator, and presumably anyone else they encounter. The striking internal rhymes of these last two lines emphasize the horror of what is happening, reinforcing the striking visual images: "gowns" and "rounds" both rhyme, while the internal rhyme of "briars" and "desires" highlights the ways in which the poet is being harmed by the thorny briars which the priests are imprisoning him with. We can picture him bound up in a thorny bush of rules and regulations. In such a way, we are able to see that Blake is constructing a picture of what the world of experience looks like both on a visual and metaphorical level.

This last sentence is important because it manages to utilise my evidence to answer the question. Many students tend to provide good textual analysis but often fail to relate it to the question in hand. Always keep the question at the back of your mind, making sure that all your points are, in some or another, answering it, or building up an argument which does answer it. This is my next section:

> The priest's "briars" are very similar to the "mind-forged manacles" that he says he "hears" in *London*. They are, of course, not literal "briars" but metaphorical ones which "tangle" up its victim in a series of prohibitions or "bans" -- as Blake describes them in London. The world of experience for Blake is full of "taboos" which colonise the minds of the

inhabitants of the world of experience. It is clear from *The Garden of Love* and from *London*, that the worst thing that "experienced" people suffer from is the lack of intellectual freedom and the voices of authority in their heads which tell them that "joy" and the expression of "desire" is sinful.

In contrast, Blake reveals the world of innocence to be a place without prohibitions. A parallel poem to *The Garden of Love* in his *Songs of Innocence* is *The Ecchoing Green* which describes in three short verses the morning, afternoon and night-time of a perfect yet realistic world. The children "sport" on the green, while the skies are "happy"; "old folk" watch the children kindly, remembering how they felt the joy of youth as they look on. In the evening, the parents of the children gather the children in like "birds in the nest".

For all Blake's depiction of a rural idyll, his pre-lapsarian "innocent" paradise is tempered by hard-headed realism. We learn at the end of the poem that the green is not "ecchoing" but "darkening"; the dactylic quality of this word, which has a heavy stress on the first syllable followed by two lighter stresses, creates a falling effect. It is as if this innocent world is falling into a world of darkness and death. Blake's world of innocence then is a world which more than acknowledges the fact of death -- the transience of life. Furthermore, it actually celebrates transience; there is an awareness from the old folk that childhood joys were fleeting but intense. Blake repeats the adverb "such" to create the intense effect of the "old folks'" remembrance: "such, such were the joys". The "old folk" remember fondly and intensely because they are aware these moments of joy have passed. In other poems, Blake is at pains to emphasize the transience of joy in the world of innocence. In *Infant Joy*, we are invited to revel in the fleeting moments that all of us enjoy as very young babies. In *Blossom* and *Spring* we are aware that the concentrated moments when nature blooms disappear very quickly.

Songs of Innocence and Experience: A Study Guide

The imagery of these poems is inter-laced with visions of transience and fleetingness: the "sound of the flute", the "soft wool" of the lamb, the "bosom" of the blossom are all transitory sensations enjoyed by the innocent mind. Thus, we could argue that Blake is postulating the case that in a world of innocence, people are allowed to enjoy the moment and are aware of the temporality of the world; this is not a world which is "fixed" and "frozen" by rules and regulations. People can enjoy their innocence because they do not have "priests in black gowns" regulating their thoughts and actions by telling them "thou shalt not".

In such a way, we can see that Blake's primary technique is to "actualize" and "realize" a deeply philosophical point about human consciousness in a poetic form. His purpose, at root, is didactic: he is aiming to educate us about innocence and experience by immersing us in these two different worlds. He uses his illuminated art to enhance and add to this immersive experience. As we read all the poems in the collection we become aware by the means of repeated images of the essential components of innocence and experience. Innocence, as we have already seen, is characterised by an ability to live with joy in the moment; it is a state of mind rather than a physical place. *The Ecchoing Green* can be found by all of us when we "sport", when we leave our rules and regulations behind; when we laugh, sing and revel in the joys of nature and each other. Equally, "experience" is a dark, wintry psychic place; it is a state of mind, which is constantly censoring one's desires. So we can perceive that Blake's poetic techniques are serving a profound didactic purpose.

Without fully knowing it, the reader is being inducted into two different states of mind as he or she reads the two books. As our minds conjure up the rural idyll of *The Lamb*, *The Shepherd*, and *The Ecchoing Green*, we are, whether we know it or not, creating "innocent" moments for ourselves; we are part of Blake's world of innocence. Equally, as we feel the injustice and imprisonment of the "briars" and "mind-forged manacles" of The Garden of Love and London, we are residing in the world of experience. Blake's technique then is not to lecture us, but to paint verbal pictures and stories which have an immersive effect; we learn to "be" innocent and experienced as we read the poems, and the imagery remains and lingers in our minds. Because the poems are so memorable, deploying as they do striking rhythms, strident rhymes, and startlingly fresh images, we find the more we read the poems the more they live inside us.

This is the first draft of my essay. I have written it, after doing some planning, more or less "off the cuff"; following a train of thought. It is not perfect. There are places where I could back up my points with more evidence and analysis if I so wished. The important thing for students to learn though is that I did allow room to discover things as I wrote the essay; I wasn't fully aware until I had written the essay that Blake is attempting to provide an "immersive" experience, trying to get us to "feel" innocence rather than intellectually examine it. Another thing that should come through is my enthusiasm and passion for the poetry. This is vital. Really good answers will be energetic and full of genuine love of the poetry; they will examine the experience of reading and appreciating literature. That is not to say that you should be saying that you love the poetry and it's absolutely marvellous, rather you should be revealing through intellectual discussion that the literature has a powerful effect upon the reader; it makes you feel, think and see things.

Bibliography

Ackroyd, P. (1999) *Blake* Vintage, London.
Bedard, M. (2006) *William Blake: The Gates of Paradise* Tundra Books, New York.
Bentley, G. (2003) *The Stranger from Paradise: a biography of William Blake.* Yale University Press. USA.

Blake, W. (edited Grant & Johnson) (2008) *Blake's Poetry and Designs: Norton Critical Editions*. W.W. Norton & company, USA.
Blake, W. & Keynes, G. (1970) *Songs of Innocence and Experience: Shewing the Two Contrary States of the Human Soul, 1789-1794*. Oxford University Press. UK.
Crehan, S. (1984) *Blake in Context*. Gill & McMillan. London.
Gilchrist, A & Holmes, R. (1863/2005) *Gilchrist on Blake – Classic Biographies edited by Richard Holmes*. Harper Perennial, London.
Foster-Damon, S. (1979) *A Blake Dictionary*. Revised edition. Universtiy of New England.
Eaves, M. (2003) *The Cambridge Companion to William Blake*. Cambridge University Press. UK.
Erdman, D. (1977) *Blake: Prophet Against Empire: A Poet's Interpretation of the History of His Own Times*. Princeton University Press, USA.
Frye, N. (1947) *Fearful Symmetry*. Princeton University Press, USA.
Leader, Z. (1981) *Reading Blake's Songs*. Routledge and Kegan Paul. London.
Marsh, N. (2012) *William Blake: The Poems (Analysing Texts)*. Palgrave MacMillan. UK.

About the author

Francis Gilbert is a writer who has been a secondary school teacher for over twenty years in various London schools. He has published numerous books, including *I'm A Teacher, Get Me Out Of Here* and *The Last Day of Term* as well as a series of study guides on classic texts such *Frankenstein, Wuthering Heights* and *Jane Eyre* -- all published on Kindle. He currently lectures in English at a university and teaches part-time in a large comprehensive: figures 1 &2 show the A Level classes he taught Blake to. He is also currently completing a PhD in Creative Writing and Education. www.francisgilbert.co.uk

Figure 1 from left to right: Ellena Moore, Alice Mann, Tiffany Wallis (standing), Poppy Wingate (sitting), Meaghan Hayden, Harry Wellington, Francis Gilbert, Danielle Farrar, Liam Boreham, Matthew Langdon. Their display on Blake and Margaret Atwood is in the background.

Figure 2 from left to right back row: Michael Anon-Calvo, Kabir Randhawa, Nahum Johal, Harry Cannons, Hollie Dawkins, Millie Wheeler, Georgia Hussey, Britney Sullivan, Demi Donovan. Front row from left to right: Jez Etherton, Francis Gilbert, Sophie Fisher, Sarah Bonfield.

www.ingramcontent.com/pod-product-compliance
Lightning Source LLC
Chambersburg PA
CBHW030856170426
43193CB00009BA/631